After
the
Roundup

After *the* Roundup

JOSEPH WEISMANN

Translated by
RICHARD KUTNER

Indiana University Press
BLOOMINGTON & INDIANAPOLIS

This book is a publication of

Indiana University Press
Office of Scholarly Publishing
Herman B Wells Library 350
1320 East 10th Street
Bloomington, Indiana 47405 USA

iupress.indiana.edu

Original publication in French
© 2011 Michel Lafon

English translation © 2017 by
Indiana University Press

The paper used in this publication
meets the minimum requirements of
the American National Standard for
Information Sciences—Permanence
of Paper for Printed Library
Materials, ANSI Z39.48-1992.

Manufactured in the United
States of America

Cataloging information is available
from the Library of Congress.

ISBN 978-0-253-02680-4 (cloth)
ISBN 978-0-253-02691-0 (paperback)
ISBN 978-0-253-02704-7 (ebook)

1 2 3 4 5 22 21 20 19 18 17

To Joe Kogan, my fellow escapee,
who helped me to achieve the impossible

Contents

Translator's Foreword

During the night of July 16–17, 1942, twelve thousand eight hundred forty-four Jewish men, women, and children were rounded up by the French police and taken to the Vélodrome d'Hiver, a cycling stadium in Paris, where they were kept for days in unspeakable conditions before being transported in cattle cars to internment camps throughout France. Joseph Weismann, barely eleven years old, was one of them.

While my son was interviewing Joseph for an AP French class he was teaching on the Holocaust, Joseph asked him if he knew anyone who could translate his memoir, *Après la rafle*, into English. Joseph and I spoke on the phone, and I set to work. It was a moving and inspiring four months. My biggest challenges were keeping the exuberant, authentic voice of an eleven-year-old boy, adapting the 1940s Parisian street slang, and finding names for things (such as architectural features or pieces of furniture) that don't have an equivalent in English. I hope I have been successful.

The details of young Joseph's escape from the camp of Beaune-la-Rolande, after his parents and sisters were torn away from him and sent to Auschwitz, are riveting. But how would he get through the war and reconstruct his life afterward? It wasn't going to be easy or pleasant, and this memoir, written by a man of eighty through the eyes of a boy, is a testament to its author's courage, clearheadedness, positive spirit, and out-of-the-box thinking. After visiting Israel twice, the second time for two years, he decided that France, the country that had cruelly taken everything away from him and presented him with obstacles at every turn, was the only place he could make his home. How could this be?

Joseph joined the French army, married, and ran a highly successful furniture company. He had three children whom he showered with love. But until he was eighty, he kept his story bottled up inside him, giving his wife and children only the slightest hints of what had happened. It was Simone Veil, lawyer, politician, president of the European Parliament, and member of the Constitutional Council of France—herself a survivor of Auschwitz—who urged Joseph to bear witness to his experiences. That is how the original French version of this book came to be.

Roselyne Bosch's 2010 film, *La Rafle*, vividly evokes the Roundup of the Vél' d'Hiv, with Joseph as the central character. It ends with his escape. This poignant memoir, written a year later, tells the rest of the dramatic story.

It was Joseph's fervent desire to write *After the Roundup* in the hope that history wouldn't repeat itself. Let's hope that his wish is fulfilled.

Richard Kutner

After
the
Roundup

1 · Fall 1940

Time to go. I slip on my jacket, plant a kiss on Mama's cheek—just a quick peck—and zoom down the stairs full speed ahead. I've made it about two flights when I hear a shout of exasperation behind me: "Joseph! Every morning. . . . The door!"

But I forget Papa's reproach right away. I cross the dark, narrow courtyard, fly across the tile floor of the front building, and push open the heavy wooden door. I'm outside at last, a smile on my face. My hair, light as a feather, flies in the wind, and I hop like a bird from one corner to the next. An early morning shower has left the paving stones shiny and slippery. The shopkeepers are raising their heavy metal gates, even if they have nothing to sell, and an old man in filthy blue work clothes is pushing his cart to the top of the hill. Montmartre is my garden. All the way to the left, Rue Lepic snakes its way uphill. I'll arrive at my destination right after the bend in the road. On my way to school, I meet up with my friend Guéchou.

"Hey! I need to talk business with you . . . something I thought of to earn a little money!"

He stares at me with wide-open eyes but not much enthusiasm. He doesn't even seem skeptical, no less worried—I've barely aroused his curiosity.

"What kind of business? And what do you need money for, anyway?"

"To buy candy, of course. Have you eaten a lot of candy lately? It's been ages since I tasted a *berlingot*!"

"That's for sure, but in these times . . . . And how do you think you're going to go about this?"

We arrive at school. I schedule a meeting at playtime to put the finishing touches on my plan.

My schoolbag has been feeling heavier and heavier. Now, in the fall of 1940, it doesn't contain any more books or notebooks than it did last year. It's my back that's having trouble bearing the load. I'm nine and a half and as fragile as a sparrow. For more than a year now I haven't had enough to eat every day. The past few weeks have been even worse, with the rationing tickets. I'm in the J2 category, kids ages six to twelve. In theory, we have the right to seven ounces of bread a day, a little sugar (or rather saccharine), one or two potatoes, and a half a steak per week. I say in theory because even with your ticket in your hand, it isn't easy to exchange it for food. The shopkeepers keep their provisions for themselves or sell them on the black market. My family doesn't have enough money to buy things that way. And I think that even if we did, we wouldn't. It's a matter of principle. My family respects the rules, whatever they may be. We obey the laws of the country that has welcomed us—I'd even say that we submit to them completely. We want to walk with our heads held high and not be ashamed of anything. We don't fool around—except for me.

"So listen, Guéchou. We're going to earn some money. I'm not asking you to steal, don't worry. We're going to earn it by starting a small business. What do you say?"

He makes a face, thrusting his hands in his pockets. "I say that we don't have much to sell."

"There must be something to sell in your house. Something pretty that people would like but that your parents don't really want to keep, no?"

"I can't think of anything."

"Wait a minute, Guéchou! I've got an idea! You must have some postcards. . . . "

"Postcards? Uh . . . yeah, I have some, but there's stuff written on the back."

"Of course there's stuff written on the back, but who cares? What counts is the picture. Do you have some nice ones? Landscapes, mountains, rivers, churches?"

"Uh, yeah, sure, but they're all in the drawer of the kitchen hutch. I don't really think I can have them."

"Don't ask!"

"Don't ask? And what if I get caught?"

"OK, ask. Will you be able to convince your mother to give them to you?"

"It depends. To do what?"

He doesn't see what I'm getting at, this pal of mine. Suddenly I wonder why I chose him of all people to go into business with me. The little voice in my head stops me right away: *Don't wonder why, Joseph. He's your best friend, that's all.*

"Listen, Guéchou," I explain, "you know, lots of people collect postcards. They remind them of somewhere they went on vacation before the war. Some people tape them to their bedroom walls. They think they're traveling when they fall asleep at night. . . ."

Finally, my friend's face lights up.

"And some people want their buddies to think that they have rich friends who wrote to them!"

"Right, Guéchou. You finally understood. For one reason or another, everyone likes postcards. So tonight you go home, you gather what you have, I do the same, and Thursday we go into business!"

We choose the central island in the Boulevard Clichy, between the Blanche and Anvers subway stations. The Place Clichy is too close to my house, and Sacré-Coeur is even worse. Here, at least, we won't be spotted. Because, of course, we know we're doing something illegal, especially Guéchou. He leans against a tree as if he wants to disappear inside its trunk.

"No, Joe, I can't. *You* start. I swear, I can't do it."

"Guéchou, you're just chicken."

I take a deep breath and address the passersby. "Excuse me, sir, wouldn't you like a postcard? Look at this one—it's Givors. Givors is beautiful! Madam, a nice postcard? No? Have a nice day, madam. Sir, have you ever been to Givors?"

The black-and-white photo shows a factory next to a river. The employees, in their white smocks, are on a break. I wait a while and realize that this particular postcard is not going to stimulate a lot of interest. Maybe I'll be more successful with the hot springs at Évian.

"Sir, how about a postcard to decorate your living room? It's Évian, a beautiful town, Évian."

The gentleman smiles at me politely as a big hand, which I imagine as huge as it is powerful, lands on my shoulder.

"Hey, kid. What are you doing?"

It's a policeman. A policeman accompanied by another policeman. All together, two policemen. I size up the situation. Two policemen: That makes two men, as many as Guéchou and me. Except that we look like two baby birds that just fell out of their nest . . . while they seem more like two adult raptors. Each is wearing a long, dark cape over his uniform. You could hide ten kids my size inside. While the big one with the mustache is grabbing me by the collar, I imagine that he's going to slip me quickly into the thick fabric and that I'm going to disappear forever. Guéchou, who's standing off to the side, doesn't even seem to have the presence of mind to run off as if we don't know each other. On the contrary, he moves closer to me.

I mumble, "Um ... Mr. Policeman, sir ... it's just postcards of Givors. Nice, no? No. ... How about Évian?"

"Young man, do you have a permit?"

"A what?"

"OK, off to the precinct. Your parents will come get you there."

The look on my father's face when he sees me. . . . He's just sorted out my fate with the police officers while Guéchou and I were waiting in an office, biting our nails. He doesn't say a word. I keep my mouth shut, too. I immediately lost my gift of gab on the way to the precinct with Guéchou. From then on, I didn't say a single word.

I follow Papa silently—completely out of character for me— and his silence communicates his shame to me more effectively than words ever could. There's not much to explain and nothing to say to justify my actions. I, Joseph Weismann, have been apprehended by the authorities for committing a crime on a public thoroughfare. And I know full well that in my family, we don't fool around.

I know it, but I don't yet know why.

The last time I had candy, it was because of a business deal as well. Outside my building, two yards from the Italian flower seller who sets up her stand when the weather is nice, I found a rubber band. And I sold it, or almost. My potential client gave me fifty *centimes*, but he let me keep the rubber band. I went to buy some *roudoudous*, rolled-up licorice with a piece of candy in the center. The candy changes color as you suck on it. I would have shared them with my sisters, but the little voice in my head warned me: *Joseph, if you bring these things home, your parents are going to ask you how you got them. They'll think you stole money from them, or worse, that you were begging. It will open a huge can of worms.* . . . I listened to my conscience, for better or worse. But I felt so pathetic eating these candies in secret, hidden away in the park, that they tasted bitter to me.

I live at 54 Rue des Abbesses, Paris, eighteenth *arrondisse-ment*. It's a simple, working-class neighborhood, where people from all different countries live. I rub shoulders with them every day, in the street, at school, outside my building, or in the park where I play with my friends. For a while now, there's been a sign up at the entrance to the park: "NO JEWS ALLOWED." I go there, anyway. Does anyone even know I'm Jewish?

Around here people don't stay cooped up in their houses, reclining on long couches, protected by heavy velvet curtains. . . . Our modest apartments don't lend themselves to that sort of thing. The inhabitants of Montmartre are so different from one another that in the end they form a whole, a multicolored mass of hardworking men and women. Behind them trail a bunch of skinny, happy kids like me. What difference does it make if you're black, yellow, or white? And who cares about your religion, if you have one? I, in any case, never think about it, and neither do Guéchou, Bedèze, Raymond, Charret, or any of my other friends.

Every day I kiss my mother before I leave to meet up with them at school. My sisters, Charlotte and Rachel, have already gone off in the other direction, toward the Rue Houdon. They never run the risk of arriving breathless at the gate of the school and having their ears pinched by the principal. I kiss my mother because she's what I love most in the world. I kiss her just for the pleasure of feeling her cheek next to mine, without another thought, and I head out on my adventures.

Whoever thought up school didn't have me in mind. I don't like to stay sitting for long. The poetry the teacher recites does nothing for me—it has no music. I have fun with words when I'm talking and also pretty much when I'm writing. I have a quick repartee and write with imagination. I'm OK in math. I can already see that it's useful. When Papa cuts woolen fabric, with his measuring tape around his neck and his chalk in his pocket, I understand that he must have made complicated calculations. He's recorded his client's measurements, and he's drawn them onto the material, taking care to waste as little as possible.

"Joseph, take the *shmatte* and put it in the bag." A *shmatte* is a scrap of leftover fabric in Yiddish. In wartime, it can be useful.

My father reinforces the collars of our clothes with the *shmattes*. He puts patches on our elbows and knees and lengthens my shorts, which are still too short. He warns me: "Joseph, you can have whatever job you want, but don't become a tailor. It's too hard. It's always the off-season."

When he says the last two words, he pronounces them "uff-zayzun," and I haven't yet made the connection between time and business being good or bad. For years I've been wondering exactly what he's talking about. I can only guess that it doesn't augur anything good. "Zayzun" almost rhymes with "poison."

Papa doesn't have a shop with a fancy entrance and his name written in elegant letters above the door. He's just an apprentice tailor. That seems unfair to me—my father is a magician. He can take a suit so worn out that you can almost see through it and make a brand-new one. He reverses the fabric, transforms the lining, reinforces the seams. A real expert. He works in our apartment, on the fifth floor of our building, in the bigger of our two rooms. In our house you enter directly into what serves as a workshop, living room, kitchen, and bedroom for my sisters and me. No one is allowed to walk barefoot: there are pins on the floor, caught in the cracks between the boards. Once a week, magnet in hand, we get on our knees to pick them up. Every evening, we push aside the long cutting table so we can open our folding beds. Papa puts away the two irons that he always leaves on the fire and gathers up the damp cloths, the tissue paper patterns, the chalk, and the scissors, which are so big that I can't even open them. Coal is burning in the heating stove, and something simmering on the portable gas burner helps to keep our palace warm.

One day, in the Anvers park, I was talking with some guys from the fancy neighborhoods who had come to rub elbows with the common folk in Pigalle. We each drew a floor plan of our apartment in the sandy soil. One of them went on and on.

"This is the entry foyer, the dining room, and the living room just next to it that leads to the smoking room; here's the boudoir, Mama's bathroom, Papa's, a bedroom, another bedroom, and the hallway, which curves and leads to one, two, three other bedrooms. . . . "

I made them all laugh when it was my turn.

"Here's the living room-bedroom-kitchen-workshop, and there's my parents' bedroom, and that's all!"

"Don't you have a bathroom?"

"Nope, no bathroom."

I don't know if it was to console me, but the little rich boy gave me a piece of gingerbread. It was the first time I ever tasted any. Delicious!

"What about the toilet?" the most practical one in the group asked me.

"On the landing."

Sometimes I curse myself for having forgotten to pee before nightfall. The toilets are down half a flight of stairs. We share them with two old maids, who live in an apartment that I imagine is even smaller than ours, and with an old, slightly hunchbacked bachelor. He's always dressed in a gray smock, his head permanently topped with a beret, and he lives with his mother in the apartment on the left. I'm not afraid of many things—maybe even of nothing—except him. It's because of his hunchback and whatever he's hiding under his beret. I imagine a pus-filled deformity, some kind of moving, malefic growth. If I meet him in the stairway, I appeal to the little voice in my head, my adviser and most faithful friend: *Be brave, Joseph! You're small; you can slip between his legs if he tries to snatch you.*

One day I went down to the toilet just after him. I was already so far down the stairs when he closed the door that I didn't dare turn back. Once inside, I saw hundreds of little brown dots in the toilet, smaller than lentils. I was blown away. *Well, well, Joseph. So that's what a hunchback's shit looks like!* I realized years later that he had simply emptied the sawdust he used for cat litter. . . .

Papa doesn't have much to do with the neighbors. He greets them politely when he sees them and gives me a little slap on the head if I take too long to do the same. He doesn't want to make waves or—most of all—disturb anyone. Soon he'll have been in France for twenty years. He learned the language and can read and write it. He got married, had three children, and made lots of friends here. His first name is written "Schmoul" but pronounced "Schmeel," and his friends have nicknamed him Mimile, like any real Frenchman. Nevertheless, he still acts like a guest. He feels that he owes a kind of debt that he wants to pay back at all costs. Last year, as soon as war was declared, he enlisted in the army. He was almost forty and had a family—no one forced him to sign up. I didn't understand.

"Why do you want to go fight in the war, Papa?"

"I want to help my country."

"So you're going to be a soldier?"

"Not really. I can't become a French soldier because I'm not really French. The law here states that I'm still Polish because I was born in Lublin."

"Where's Lublin?"

"Now it's in Poland, but before 1918 it was in Russia."

"How can a city change countries? Paris is in France. It can't move."

"Paris won't move, but Germany wants to extend its borders to cover a big piece of Europe, including France. It's to avoid that that I want to fight."

—⁓—

So the French army—the real one, the one that hoists the tricolor flag—didn't want him. He was put in the second foreign regiment. He spent the beginning of the winter of 1939 to 1940 in the north of France before being sent with his regiment to the Free Zone in the south. He told us little about his experiences, just the following: "They fired at us with machine guns in Angoulême and Poitiers, but there were no casualties."

I told myself that if the Germans didn't learn to aim better, we would come out of the war OK. Then my father ended up in the Dordogne, in Bergerac. They needed a work force to replace the guys who had left for the front. Papa, with his delicate, magical fingers, working on a farm. . . . It turned out that a tailor could be of use in the countryside: For a few weeks he gave new life to the men's old suits and rejuvenated the women's dresses.

Like thousands of others, Mama, my sisters, and I took off along the roads of France. We walked until we came to a village in Maine-et-Loire. Two years earlier, Charlotte, Rachel, and I had vacationed for a few weeks at the home of farmers who lived near there. To shelter us until better times, these simple, good people found us a little house not far from theirs. We lived there the whole winter, trying to be as quiet as possible. We worked in the factories during the daytime, except Rachel, of course: she was only five years old. In the evening, I gathered branches in the forest that bordered the fields. I had never seen so many trees—so close together, a silent army impossible to penetrate. Crows formed black patches on the snow-covered meadows. The far-off horizon and monotonous colors made me dizzy. I missed the tall buildings and all the shades of gray in Paris. I wasn't unhappy, though. In the evening, Mama sang the same songs in Yiddish, a language I didn't understand well but which soothed me all the more. I could invent stories for them as I wished.

In June 1940 we learned that the fighting had stopped, and Papa arrived:

"I've been demobilized. We're going back home."

I never understood if he was happy or unhappy. If the war was over, and if Papa had come back safe and sound, we should rejoice, shouldn't we? Our friends watched us leave and made a thousand promises: "You're not alone. You can count on us. We won't forget you."

Finally back together, Mama, Papa, my sisters, and I took the train with thousands of other Parisians returning to their homes, torn between disappointment at the French defeat and relief at the return to peacetime. The train car was packed with people. Papa sat on the steps for the whole trip back. I was trembling all over. What if he fell off or was hurt or killed? . . .

At the Gare Montparnasse we piled all our belongings in a cart and walked and walked and walked to the Butte Montmartre, in the very north of Paris. Our feet were bleeding when we crossed the threshold of our apartment. Night had fallen on the city and on us. During the months of the war when we weren't there, nothing had really changed in the neighborhood. It was springtime now—a spring a little gloomier than the previous ones, but spring just the same. The greengrocers had nothing to sell on their stands, the tools in the hardware store no longer seemed to interest anyone, the tinsmiths were idle. Since there was nothing to cook in the pots and pans, why repair them?

The farmers in Bergerac had good memories of Papa. His new friends encouraged him to stay there with his wife and children: "There's lots of room," they assured him, "and you'll have more to eat here than in Paris." No doubt from an excess of discretion, he refused. The people from Périgord didn't forget us, though. Throughout the summer, even into October, they sent us plump chickens regularly in the mail. But now, at the end of 1940, winter is coming. It's getting colder and colder, we're hungrier and hungrier, and the chickens have been replaced by beets before they can reach us. I'm outraged by this injustice.

"Papa, you're not going to say anything to the postal employees? They have the right to steal our chickens?"

"No, Joseph. I'm simply going to write to our friends to thank them sincerely for their packages, but I'll tell them that it's no use sending any more."

⁓

Papa never protests against anyone or anything. He doesn't engage in debates—he doesn't like politics. But he reads the newspaper every day. He sends me to buy it, at the *tabac* next to our building.

"Get me the *Pariser Zeitung*, Joseph. If I read a German newspaper, I'll find out more than if I read a French one."

He certainly seems to discover news, but it gives him no pleasure. The Germans are advancing, and my father, in an increasingly sullen mood, goes out on Sundays to meet his friends in a café in the Rue Cauchois, where they play *belote*, a card game. I don't ask him many questions, so I don't distress him further, but I follow him to the bar. I hope to learn more by listening to his discussions with his pals. Usually in vain. Papa smokes his Gauloise in silence. He plays his cards skillfully, but he quickly tires of the fiery debate going on around the table.

"Come, Joseph. We're going home."

"Listen, Mimile, don't get angry! The war, the Germans, Marshal Pétain—it's all part of life."

"It's all politics, and it's no good for us."

Out in the street, Papa smiles at me, so for once I dare to ask a question: "Papa, what's politics?"

"Politics is a lot of ideas that people stir up to make them do terrible things."

"What terrible things?"

Papa doesn't answer, and I'm left with my questions. My father is thinking about the country where he was born, which was crushed in less than a month by Hitler's army. He knows that the Bolsheviks and the Germans have each stolen their share of the land, the cities, the churches, and the synagogues—if the latter haven't been torn down. He's thinking about his brother, a member of I don't know what movement in Poland. He's thinking about the news whispered in his ear like a rumor, inconceivable even though it's from reliable sources. Horrors that are unbelievable, in the true meaning of that word. How can he believe that villages are being burned? That observant men's *payis* are being cut off, just for the pleasure of humiliating them? That their wives are forced to undress in public? That even teenage girls and elderly women are being raped with impunity? He's thinking about the young children. Someone told him that they're being thrown alive to the bottom of wells. He's thinking that humans change into animals sometimes—but animals don't treat one another like this.

I look at my father's handsome face. I know nothing of the terrible things that are distressing him so much. One glass marble is worth five clay ones. That's all I know. That's all that matters to me, and I sense that I'll be happy as long as that knowledge is enough for me.

2 · The Star

When the sleeve of one of my shirts is worn out, my father patches it with a slightly darker oval of fabric that fits right under my elbow when I bend my arm. If there's a tear in a piece of clothing, my mother grabs a needle and makes it disappear with tiny, even stitches. On this morning in May, she's busying herself with my sisters' dresses and my sweater, sewing a yellow star on the chest of each one.

My mother is an expert. She pushes in the needle less than a millimeter from the border of the star and pulls it through just at the edge. When she's finished, you could almost think that the star was part of the original fabric before it was sewn into a garment. She mumbles as she works.

Sara Gitla Weismann, née Erlichsztajn, born in 1902 in Bichawa, Poland, prays with every move she makes. If she throws a potato into the soup, she murmurs a prayer. If she remembers a happy event, she says a prayer. When she listens to my foolishness, her laughing ends with a prayer. Usually she pronounces just a few words spontaneously, barely articulated, but it doesn't matter: she said them and God heard them. They're accompanied by a quick gesture: she takes her

Star of David on its chain in her hand, raises it nimbly to her lips, and lets it drop again after a brief kiss: *"L'shanah haba'ah b'yerushalayim."*

Or, less often, the same thing in French: "Next year in Jerusalem."

At this moment, Mama's head is bent over her work. For more than an hour, I haven't been able to catch her eye. She's been sewing furiously. One can't say that a member of the Weismann family fails to follow the rules to the letter.

For a few weeks now, Papa has been using a maid's room on the seventh floor. He carried up his tools, his sewing machine, and his patterns—he's relocated his workshop in a sense. It's easier for our day-to-day living, especially when we eat our meals. But there's one major drawback: we see Papa much less often. Charlotte misses him the most. She loves to discuss things with him. Charlotte is twelve years old, the eldest, the most serious, and the proudest. She wants to pursue her studies, to learn and understand everything. She has no great ambitions, but I'm sure that she hopes to be able to improve our miserable lives. She's at the top of the class in every subject in school and is my parents' pride and joy—and I'm certainly in no position to compete with her. I never think about the future—ever. It seems to me that each day proves me right. If I think about tomorrow, I'm sure I'll find something to worry about. Charlotte and my parents' blank faces are a warning to me: something's bothering them. My philosophy is: Wait and see.

Tomorrow comes quickly. One morning in July 1942—the weather is promising but still cool—I put my jacket on, because it's already time to leave for school. This time I'm not in a hurry. In fact, today I'd prefer not to go out at all. I don't want to set foot outside until my mother removes this damned star as meticulously as she sewed it on. For once, I don't put my book bag on my back. I hold it against my body, over my heart. It's the first time I carry it with pride. The other boys have leather bags. They're not tailors' sons. My father made mine with his own hands, before I entered third grade, I remember. He spent many evenings assembling corduroy patches. . . . He said to me, "No one will have one like yours, Joseph—and no one's will be as beautiful!"

I really wanted an ordinary one. I didn't say anything to him because I didn't want to hurt his feelings. Now I suddenly realize that was the right thing to do, that I was being ridiculous. At the time I didn't want to stand out because of my book bag, and today I have a yellow star on my chest, a much more obvious sign to point out what I am. And what am I? A Jew. It must be something to be ashamed of.

The entry of our building is big enough to shelter me from the rain. It's even wide enough so that I can stand under it without blocking the way of people going in or out. I could stay there until this evening, pretending I'm waiting for someone, for example. . . . I contemplate hiding this way, knowing full well that it won't work. At any moment Papa will pass through to deliver an order, to go buy some thread at the hardware and notions store at the corner of the Rue Burq, to take his chances waiting on line at the bakery, or for some other reason. He'll see me and frown, thinking that I'm playing hooky. He won't say anything right away, but he'll look so unhappy at having a good-for-nothing son that it will be the worst possible punishment for me. Or else it will be Mama who discovers me, on the way to pick up her daughters at school. She'll moan and groan at me right in the middle of the street, with her embarrassing accent so thick you can cut it with a knife—maybe even in Yiddish—and everyone will notice us. Of course, passersby will say, "No surprise that they're creating a scene—they're Jews."

Before the war, I thought everyone was Jewish. I didn't know that I was part of a separate group, and, quite frankly, I don't know how I could have guessed. Even this morning, except for the star over my heart, I don't see what makes me different from Guéchou or the others.

I can't spend the day here. I have to make up my mind. I look for someone with a decoration similar to mine so I can walk behind him and remain invisible. When I finally find him, I can't believe my eyes: It's Raymond, big Raymond with his fat cheeks and arms twice as big as my thighs. Everyone's afraid of him, even me, but I take a chance and stop him as he passes by.

"Hey, Raymond!" I lower my book bag to my waist. He's not surprised. "Raymond, I didn't know you were Jewish. Did you know I was?"

"What difference does it make? It's nothing to be ashamed of. And there are others besides us. Come on, we're going to be late."

It's true that we're not the only ones. I spend a good part of the morning looking at my friends' shirtfronts, and then I go on to something else. My friends do the same. Among the bunch of us, being Jewish has no meaning, and neither does not being Jewish. The teacher acts as if nothing is different, either. I'd like him to teach us a class on this issue, though—to explain to us what being Jewish is. A few months ago, he pulled me aside to tell me that he had seen an exhibit on the Bolsheviks. Propaganda had already begun its work: Jews were associated with the populations of all the countries of Eastern Europe in their least appealing aspects.

"Joseph, you should have seen how these people live: They shut themselves away in hovels, they're dirty and poor, and they grunt instead of talking."

"Why are you telling me this, sir? I'm not a Bolshevik! I'm French, French from Paris. And my father comes from Poland."

"I know. But you should tell your father to go see this show. I'm sure it would interest him."

My teacher had no doubt wanted to alert us, but I didn't understand that then, and I didn't convey the message.

Another time, in the café on the Rue Cauchois, I heard my father's friends commenting about a poster that was plastered all over Paris, and which I, too, had noticed. It showed an old man with a hooked nose, long, dirty hair, and a toothless mouth. He was leaning over a globe and seemed to want to grasp the whole thing in his clawlike hands. The title was "The Jew and France." I didn't recognize myself in this caricature. It certainly didn't resemble my father, who didn't have a hair on his head, or the old men I saw at the synagogue on Saturdays. Even with their gaunt faces and long fingers, they didn't look anything like this hideous image, and their faces didn't reveal the same hateful greed. My father's friends joked about it.

"You know, Mimile, they should have chosen you as the model for their poster!"

But Papa didn't laugh.

"Come on, Mimile … it's all propaganda. You don't think the French are foolish enough to swallow all their lies, do you? We all know that Jews are no worse than anyone else."

Seated off to the side, watching them shuffle the cards and comfort Papa, I was troubled by the same sense of guilt that had gripped me that morning outside my door. Maybe I was precisely the Jew who was worse than anyone else.

I'm ashamed to be Jewish only one day a week, and that out of obligation. Every Saturday we wash ourselves more thoroughly than on other days, we dress in cleaner clothes, we spit on our shoes to make them shine, and we march off to

the synagogue. . . . Before we leave, we remove the scraps of
fabric and the sewing tools from the table. We put out our most
beautiful white tablecloth, embroidered and starched. We set
six places with our prettiest plates so everything is ready for
lunch. Six because we'll be five plus the beggar. We call him
the *schnorrer*. I hate him like poison. He gets our best food. If
we have chicken soup, we get the broth and he gets the meat.
That's why I hate him. Because we're starving, too; because
we're poor, too, yet we're giving away everything we own. This
"everything," which in reality is so little, all goes to this smelly,
filthy *schnorrer*. If that's what being Jewish is, excuse me, but
I'm not interested.

Seated in class, in my threadbare but clean clothes, even with
the yellow star sewn onto my chest, I can see that I resemble
the other kids in Montmartre, both those I like and those I
don't. Like me, in the back of their minds they must certainly
be feeling ashamed, too. In a few days, I'm going to be eleven
and start to prepare for my bar mitzvah—to please Mama and
to do my best to guarantee her a place next to God. But I worry
that I'm not worthy of this kind, good woman, who prays all
the time, and who must be praying right now, bent over a hem
or a buttonhole, that her children can grow up in peace in spite
of everything.

Paris is buzzing with rumors. I sense them more than I hear
them. They're more like signs than words. There's the kind look
of a storekeeper, a knowing wink that reminds me that I'm as
innocent as he is. There's the sign at the entrance to the park:
No Jews Allowed. I guess now Paris is at war with itself. Even
in my neighborhood, way up here in the streets surrounding
Sacré-Coeur, there are two camps waiting to confront each
other: those who have no problem with the Jews, and those
who want to ban them. As for me, I don't have a choice of which

clan I want to belong to. I just turned eleven so I've been Jewish for eleven years now. My parents began to be Jewish before me. And their own parents, whom I didn't know, before them. I could even go farther back in time, search the remotest regions of Poland, which used to part of Russia, the land of the medieval Bolsheviks my teacher described. That's where I come from, and, like them—no way to escape it—I'm Jewish. I have no idea what that means, though. I sense that a lot of people seem to know but that they have false ideas.

Papa and Mama removed the yellow stars from our sweaters very carefully and sewed them just as carefully onto our summer shirts. Each one of them cost us a fabric rationing point, which we have to be careful not to waste. . . . It's summer vacation. It's hot, and I wander around my neighborhood with Guéchou, who supports me in my misfortune. We've been banned from the élite group of kids who play in the sandbox. We don't care. We'll get over it.

At least I think so.

3 · July 16, 1942

"What are you doing outside? It's not good for Jews to be in plain sight today! Didn't anyone tell you? Go, run home to your parents!"

Papa left two hours ago. He went to take the subway, at Rue Lamarck, so he could deliver a suit to someone in the sixteenth arrondissement. Do I need to worry about him? If this man, just outside my building, told me to stay away from the Germans today, it's because the yellow stars are in danger. And obviously, Papa is wearing one. It would never occur to him not to. . . . Because those are the rules now.

I had barely climbed back upstairs to our apartment when Papa returned, still carrying the suit. Mama began to question him, visibly distressed.

"Don't worry, I'll deliver it tomorrow. A guy in the subway told me not to spend too much time outside. A factory worker, not Jewish. He approached me, at the end of the platform, with a strange look on his face, as though he was afraid someone would see him talking to me."

"A man told me to go home, too, Papa."

Charlotte raises her eyes from her book. Rachel is forming a square with her jacks and a few pebbles she must have picked up in the park. We look at one another in silence. The window overlooking the courtyard is open, and there's not a sound from the street. We can barely hear a neighbor doing her dishes, the music of the spoons banging together in the sink and of the dishes piling up in the drain board. In the next building, a baby cries for a minute, then stops. He must have fallen asleep. Mama takes up her needle again, Charlotte returns to her reading with a frown, and my little sister picks up an empty spool of thread. She slides a piece of string through the opening, attaches it to her wrist, and begins to walk an imaginary dog.

"Joseph, did you remember my cigarettes today?"

I take two cigarette butts I found on the sidewalk out of my pocket. Two dark ones and two light ones, a good harvest. Since rationing began, my father has been suffering a forced weaning from smoking that makes him suffer even more on days when he's anxious. He used to smoke Gauloise after Gauloise and now is forced to reconstitute cigarettes from butts we find in the street. The fishing is better in fancy neighborhoods. Whenever the occasion presents itself, I walk a few meters from the Germans. They exhale their smoke noisily, send their butts flying with a flick of their fingers, and I rush to pick them up. But they smoke only *blondes*, made of good Aryan tobacco, as the joke goes, and they're not Papa's favorites. He's not really fussy, though.

"Thanks, Joseph."

He opens a little metal box where he stores his cache, slips in the day's find, and takes out enough tobacco to roll a cigarette. The atmosphere is tense in our apartment. I keep walking around the table, eager to go back outside.

"Papa, can I go out? Please?"

"I don't mean to punish you, Joseph, but I think it's better for you to stay inside today. You never know."

Mama intervenes. "He's only a child. What could happen to him?"

"Papa, please! I won't hang around outside. I'll go to Charret's."

My friend lives on the Rue Constance, where his father is a shoemaker. He has a little, old shop with a red wooden boot hanging outside. You can see it from far away. It's one of the rare businesses that are not doing badly because of the war. Since it's impossible to buy new shoes, people have their old ones repaired. . . .

"Joseph, I'm sorry, but it's impossible." He smiles at me tenderly. There's nothing that will change his mind. . . . It's going to be a long day. Papa seems resigned. He spreads out a few strands of tobacco on a piece of newspaper, taking all the time he needs. He uses the same precise gestures for making his cigarette that he does for cutting out the pieces of a jacket from a roll of woolen fabric. He's right. No reason to rush today. We're not welcome in cafés or parks—we're barely accepted in the street and can wait on line at stores only at certain times. This Thursday, July 16, 1942, is just the next stage in our forced isolation from French society.

We're confined to our homes by a silent threat, urged to shut ourselves away by people we don't know. I hate them for their concern. I pour a little water in the flowerpot I put on the windowsill. Inside is a bean seed they gave me in science class. It's starting to germinate, but I don't find it to be growing very quickly. It seems as bored as the rest of us. I flop into a chair with a sigh. Papa kisses Mama on the forehead and leaves. We hear his footsteps in the stairway climbing up to the seventh floor, then the door of his little workshop closing. The baby starts to cry again—but is it the same one? Charlotte is turning the pages of her book, and Rachel has caught her dog's leash in the table legs. I think I hate the Germans even more than the *schnorrer.*

—⁓—

Around noon there's a knock at our door. The table is set, and Mama has been standing over a pot for the last few minutes. All our eyes converge on her with a questioning look. It can't be Papa—he would have entered quietly. Two more knocks. Charlotte goes to answer the door and immediately steps back. A uniformed policeman and a man in civilian clothes come in quickly and rush to the window to close it.

"Madame Weismann?"

"Yes, that's me. Why are you closing the window? It's hot!"

"Several women have thrown themselves onto the sidewalk already today. We don't want another incident."

They're dressed in black, and even on a stormy, humid day like today, the police officer is wearing his cape.

"Get your things—a few articles of clothing and enough food for two days. You're under arrest."

"You're arresting me?"

"The children, too."

The other man, who up to now hasn't said a word, asks, "Where's your husband?"

Mama hesitates, or else she didn't understand—I don't know which. She holds Rachel against her legs and mumbles something in Yiddish, so quietly that none of us can hear it.

Suddenly the cop shouts, "Where is he?"

My mother's incredulous look suddenly turns toward me. "Joseph, go get Papa."

I move toward the door under the gaze of the two increasingly impatient men.

"Pack your things. And hurry up!"

By the time Papa and I get down to the fifth floor, our miserable boiled cardboard suitcases are already packed. We have several, but they're all small. They look ready to burst, as though if we lift them by their handles, the bottoms are going to give way, and our belongings will be scattered all over the floor. A few articles of clothing and enough food for two days, that's what they said. I'm not even sure that the soup is ready for tonight. What do these morons think? That my parents are hiding cans of beans under their mattress? That some breaded turkey cutlets are waiting patiently to be sautéed in a pan? That our cabinets are filled with jars of jam? What cabinets? We don't even have any! *Joe, don't lose your temper. And don't think about food: that'll get you even more upset. . . .* Papa seems so calm. He caresses Mama's shoulder and comforts Charlotte with a nod of his head that means "Don't worry, I'm here. Everything will be OK—I'm in control of the situation."

My poor father's not in control of anything. He lifts his head and sticks out his chest. Although he's not tall, he pulls himself up to his full height to show everyone that he's not afraid. That he'll keep his dignity whatever happens, because he's an honest man with nothing to reproach himself for.

"Gentlemen, where are we going?"

"You'll see when we get there. Follow us."

"I fought in the war for France, sir. I certainly have the right to know where you're taking us!"

"A bus is waiting for us downstairs. What happens after that, we don't know. Those are our orders, that's all."

At school, when a classmate refuses to do something that requires a little courage, we say he's chicken. I can sense that this police officer belongs to the next category, the worst: the real cowards. He wants us to believe that he's only following orders. And he takes us for a bunch of idiots. To be sure, he's following orders, but he knows where we'll be spending the night. I can already imagine him safe and warm in his bed.

We grab our cardboard suitcases and close the door behind us. Immediately, one of the men places a wax seal on the door-frame, another on the wooden panel, and stretches a ribbon between the two. I don't know exactly what this thing is; I don't understand—except that we'll have to pull it all down to get back into our apartment.

Our procession begins to make its way down the stairs. A silent procession, punctuated only by the sound of our torn-up shoes on the wooden steps. Our guards must have better soles than ours: their shoes make sharper sounds, louder, crisper. It looks as though we're the only Jews at 54 Rue des Abbesses, or at least the only ones being arrested. The concierge's little room is closed. We hardly know Madame Auger. She's a dis-creet woman who conscientiously sweeps the hallways and the courtyard and keeps track of who enters the building during the night. On her door is written: "Please give your name after 10:00 p.m." Since the curfew began, it's been a long time since anyone has gone out at night, though.

I'm finally outside, but not the way I had hoped. I feel as though I'm in one of my comic strips. Give yourselves up, you're surrounded! Only this time it's a lot less funny. My parents' faces . . . expressionless, defeated, desperate. . . . Papa is serious, and Mama is crying in silence. In Charlotte's eyes, however, I can detect anger. She's furious at being taken away, enraged at this offense to her family. She holds her breath, her chin thrust forward slightly, jaw tense as if she were ready to bite someone. I seem to be seeing her for the first time. So my big sister is not just an annoying girl, always too well behaved to disobey—even to have the idea enter her head? And me? Joseph, who brags all the time, the eleven-year-old rascal who doesn't even weigh 65 pounds, who can run hundreds of yards behind the milk truck and not be outdistanced? . . . I should have saved my energy: no cheese ever fell out, and now I'm a prisoner like the others.

We walk toward the Place des Abbesses, indifferent to the passersby, who don't look at us, either. I try to see myself through their eyes. What kind of spectacle are we providing for the grocers, the tobacco sellers, the deliverymen whom we've frequented every day for years? The image of a hopeless family, shoulders bent, eyes filled with tears. Accompanied by two good Frenchmen appointed by the Vichy government, one in front and the other behind—two honest, upright men who don't doubt for a moment the usefulness of their mission— we're five doomed people carrying, in our pitiful cardboard suitcases, the little—so little—we've ever possessed.

When we get to the corner of Rue Durantin, we stop for a moment. It suddenly occurs to me that I could take off in a flash, up to the top, in the labyrinth of stairs that climb up to Sacré- Coeur. I can run fast, and by the time the two guards decide which of them has the responsibility to catch me, I'll already be far away. . . . I don't do it. I look at my dear mother and father, both of them so distraught; I look at Rachel, hanging onto Charlotte like a shipwrecked person to his raft. I feel no stronger, no less worried than they. And, quite simply, I love them. Honestly, what would I do without them? I get into the bus.

—※—

We don't make this trip alone. On the way, the driver picks up several other families escorted by the police. So many people are rounded up that there isn't enough room for everyone to sit. Parents place their little ones on their laps, and we leave the seats for the old. We're ushered into the town hall of the eighteenth arrondissement, where other Jewish families are waiting, with their stars on their chests and the same suitcases at their feet. From there, we have to board another bus. No one says a word until the vehicle stops, and a man standing in the front exclaims, "It's the Vélodrome d'Hiver! I recognize it. It's the Vélodrome d'Hiver!"

And so it is.

The bus parks in front of the entrance, and we're too dejected to annoy our guards with questions. But what's going to happen now? Papa wipes his brow every two minutes, the women's foreheads are glistening, and the men have large sweat stains under their arms. Not unusual—it's hot, the sky is getting dark, and you can feel a storm approaching.

I've never been inside the Vélodrome d'Hiver, but I know what usually goes on there. I've often read about boxing matches or bicycle races there in the newspaper. When I was first learning to read, it was good practice. I would sit under a table at Père Fabri's, Papa would play belote, and I would decipher the words on the sports pages. So this is where it all happened. . . . I doubt that we've all been brought here to enjoy a sporting event.

Two more vehicles park behind us in the Rue Nélaton. Maybe we've been waiting for them. Anyway, it's time. They make us get out. Special security officers already there form a line on each side of the street. We proceed down the sidewalk and make our way through a passageway that ends at a pair of wide swinging doors. People are crying all around me—children, too, probably. I don't know: I can't see very much since I'm only four feet six. All I can see are bent backs, worn-out pants seats, leather belts around women's dresses soaked with sweat, and stretched-out sweaters, completely useless in this heat.

We go in and are assaulted by a deafening tumult. Instinctively, we move closer to one another. There are five of us: Papa, Mama, Charlotte, Rachel, and me. But we're only one body compared to the ear-splitting mass before us. Pushed from the rear, we move ahead until the doors close behind us: today's delivery, several dozen people, three busloads.

I never realized that the Vélodrome was so big. I could have never imagined that it contained so many rows of bleachers, so wide and so high. And I certainly wouldn't have guessed that once all the seats were occupied, the space could continue to be filled with human beings—exactly like stuffing a suitcase with shirts that you're not afraid of wrinkling. But shirts don't feel anything. They don't need air to breathe; they don't need to stretch their legs or lie down. Whether they're old or new, it doesn't matter: They don't feel pain. For them, human dignity doesn't exist.

Mama exclaims fearfully, "How many of us are there in here?"

Throughout the month of May, there were rumors around Paris that hundreds of Jews had been arrested. Policemen had knocked on their doors, just like at our house a short while ago, and taken the men away.

Papa commented on the situation, trying to reassure us: "Yes, I know that there are roundups, but they're not for insignificant people like us. They're for important Jews—Blum, Mendès France. And it's the intellectuals that the Germans fear the most. But the rest of us. . . . They're not threatened by us, the tailors, the painters, the shoemakers, the chair caners, the penniless workers. So it's logical that we're not running any risk with them, either!"

It's 3:30 in the afternoon in the Vélodrome. Papa was wrong. Obviously, since this morning, there have been buses, there have been deliveries of Jews, and not only politicians and university professors. Families like ours, insignificant people like us, plenty of them. We're among our own kind here, and there are thousands of us.

—⁓—

We need to find a place to sit. At first, we don't dare spread ourselves out too much. First of all, we don't know how long we're going to be here. But as the evening wears on, we sense that we're probably going to spend the night in this place. And other convoys continue to arrive. The doors swing open at a regular pace, and the men in their capes push dozens of people into the Vélodrome. Unwittingly, they form a mirror into the past for us: They have the same stunned look on their faces that we had a few hours ago. Like us, they're going to scatter in the aisles and the different levels. Like us, they're going to thank a family who moves over to make room for them. Like us, they're going to take out their bread, divide it into enough pieces for each of them, and, as it was for us, this bread won't satisfy their hunger. Nothing will ease their pain.

The storm finally breaks. Drops of rain as heavy as artillery shells begin to fall on the glass roof. For a few minutes, their sound covers all the sobs, the shouts, the wailing, the prayers. A woman comments quietly, as if to herself, "It's God crying over the fate of the Jews."

We lose track of how much time has passed. The glass ceiling has been made opaque so as not to be visible during the bombings. There are neon lights that give off a yellow glow. Night falls, but it's as bright as daytime.

"Joseph, walk around and try to find your uncles."

"Émile and Albert? You think they're here, Mama? You really think so?"

"There are so many Jews! Why not them?" She shrugs her shoulders, resigned. She hopes that they're here, too. We could group together. They might have some food to share with us. She hopes just as much that they escaped being rounded up. Mama doesn't know what to hope for.

I go off on my hunt. I search the bleachers, one by one, from the top to the bottom. I see women, lots of them, with babies asleep in their arms. I notice one who's pregnant rocking back and forth as if she wants to soothe the baby in her womb. I see bodies intertwined, legs, feet, arms, and a few heads emerging from the pile. They're alive, though: I can see them moving from time to time, gently so as not to disturb anyone. But that old woman over there, completely slumped over . . . with her head resting on her own shoulder. It's an impossible position to get into. I try to reproduce it without success. I must not be limber enough. Or dead enough. Is that what happens when your heart stops beating? You get all limp? *Better get going, Joe. Don't forget: it's Albert and Émile that you're looking for.*

There are plenty of things to look at, though. Some people are dressed any old way. You can see that they put on all the clothes they could get their hands on when the police came to take them away. Some remain seated, their backs as stiff as ramrods. They don't want to give in. They don't cry or complain, and they still find the strength to pray. They're the oldest ones here. Below, on the bicycle track, the Red Cross has set up tents. Nurses in white blouses go in and out endlessly. They listen to people's complaints, distressed and helpless. It smells really bad in the farthest reaches of the stadium, against the walls, especially at the very top. The toilets are all clogged, so people relieve themselves everywhere. I tell myself that if my uncles are here, they certainly can't have chosen these places to sit. From now on, I'm avoiding them.

It takes me three hours to search the entire Vélodrome. When I return to Mama, I don't need to say a word. A vague shake of the head is enough of an answer.

"Come, Joseph. Go to sleep."

Rachel is taking up all the space in her lap. I squat on the floor. It takes a long time before I finally fall asleep.

—⁂—

We've been here for three days. No one else has entered, and no one has left. Except the bodies. I don't pay any attention. I'm not afraid for my parents. They're young and strong, and they have no diseases. I feel confident, and it's good to feel in the bottom of my heart that nothing can happen to us. I haven't made any friends. I see a small group of boys down on the track. They're not running or playing. They're all a little exhausted. It's unbearably hot. The adults don't move from the bleachers. There aren't too many of them praying anymore, and yet there's a lot of noise all the time. Papa says you'd think you were in a beehive. It's unbelievable, after all the time we've been trapped in here, with no news from outside and nothing to do all day long, that people still find things to talk about. Actually, by talking nonstop, people feel reassured. They come up with hypotheses. They're amazed that there are so many of us here and are sure that our numbers make us less vulnerable. They give one another news of a neighbor, a cousin, a friend: They've wandered around the Vélodrome several times, even after the doors were completely shut. This neighbor, that cousin, this friend isn't with us. He must be somewhere else. He's not as hungry or thirsty as we are. Now we're sure: those that weren't rounded up are the lucky ones.

"I'm not worried!" an old man shouts. "I heard they're taking us to a camp, in the east, where each of us can practice his trade."

Another, not much younger, bursts out laughing: "And you believe that?"

"Why not? What else could they do with us? We're just waiting here."

"Waiting for what?"

"Waiting for them to find us our own land, a country just for us. You can laugh at me, take me for the old fool that I am maybe. It's clear to me that they don't want us here anymore— but it's a big world out there."

"It may be a big world, but for two thousand years we haven't been welcome anywhere. Don't kid yourself. . . ."

"You have to hope. What else can you do? Where? Where could we go?"

"It's always the same old question, my friend. . . ."

Mama listens to the conversation but doesn't say a word. She caresses our arm or our hair whenever we're within her reach. Otherwise, she remains seated, immobile, weak, ashamed. Papa talks less and less. Charlotte is sulking as if she's angry. You'd think that she's afraid she'll never see her books again. Rachel, the youngest, cries more and more often. As for me . . . I'm waiting like everyone else. I've woven an opaque cloak in my head, a cloth that covers the five of us, that keeps us together, separate from the thousands of others surrounding us. I'm a wasp that someone turned a glass over. I'm not wasting my energy banging into the sides of the glass. I'm calm but alert. I spend my days holding my breath because it stinks so much in here, but I keep telling myself that we're still together as a family, and that's what's important.

We've met so many women who are looking for children who had gone out to play when they were arrested. They imagine them lost, alone—they look terribly distressed. In any case, I think it's the mothers who are suffering the most. Suffering for their children who are being starved, suffering for not being able to care for them, suffering from the lack of hygiene and privacy. I don't know where they get their strength. Mama is like the rest—disheveled, bedraggled, dirty. These are women who never stepped a foot out of their homes without putting their hair neatly in a bun and straightening their clothes, because the least you can do is make yourself presentable when you're so poor. Now they don't care what they look like. They don't even think about it anymore, don't ask themselves any questions. They feel silent pity for the fate of their loved ones, not for themselves. Only once I hear an uproar. There's a loud thud followed by shouts that fill the entire space: "A woman just threw herself from the top of the bleachers!"

For many long minutes everyone reflects on what has just happened. Someone asks me, "Joseph? Joseph? Are you all right?"

I don't answer. I've cut myself off from the drama happening all around me.

—⁓—

For two days, people have been leaving. Policemen have passed through the aisles, coordinating the departure of several hundred families in an orderly, methodical way. Apparently it's not going fast enough. A voice, projected by the loudspeakers, announces the imminent departure of the last of us. And we still number in the thousands.

"Gather your belongings! All of you are leaving in ten minutes! Go to the main door."

Relief is mixed with panic. Exhausted by five days without eating or drinking—or very little, anyway—many of them struck with dysentery, the adults gather their last strength to pack up the linens they brought, still perfumed with lavender but reeking of excrement now, like our skin and our hair. The little ones have snotty noses, dirty behinds, faces full of red spots. They have measles, scarlet fever, chicken pox, and I don't know what other diseases. It's so hot under the glass roof, and their fever is so high. . . . It's as though they're burning from inside. I hear people say, "Finally! They haven't forgotten us. It doesn't matter where they're taking us. It can't be worse than here."

Others sigh, "Maybe we'll be able to wash ourselves. . . ."

And others, excited, add:

"And take care of our children."

"And eat something. Or drink . . . just something to drink."

Crushed together by men in uniform, like the day of our arrival, we're shoved into buses, unceremoniously but without real violence. There must be some kind of urgency, even though we've been marinating for several days in our own filth and sweat.

Just like last Thursday, we climb into the vehicles, with no idea where they're going to take us. We have the same skeptical looks on our faces as when we arrived: There are so many of us. What are they going to do with us? There are people so old that they can't walk anymore. What's to become of them? Will they leave them here? No, they have to be carried. There are people so sick that they can't get up. They're taken away, too. We don't know what's going on because no one tells us. Besides, it's getting harder and harder to catch the eye of a policeman.

At first they weren't very friendly, but at least they answered us when we asked questions. They'd say, "I don't know," or "You'll see." But now they ignore us completely. As if we don't speak the same language. As if they don't hear us. As if they resent having to be here, having to watch over us now, when we're so repulsive. But what can we do? It's because of them that we're in this state!

When we finally step outside—even if it's only for two minutes, the time it takes to walk the few meters separating the Vélodrome from the bus—I throw the protective cloak that I invented over us. I take a deep breath. I look to my right, to my left, behind me, in front of me: everywhere the same desolation, but I can finally fill my lungs with air, with freedom, with life. An ordeal has ended; we all survived.

―――

From the Vélodrome d'Hiver we're taken to the Gare d'Austerlitz railroad station. It's crawling with police, armed men—all French. But that's not all: Germans are waiting for us on the platforms in impressive numbers, every five meters, holding back huge dogs on leashes. They're wearing their decorations for the occasion: large plaques hanging from their chests, over their pretty brass buttons: *Feldwebel*, they say. The pieces of metal are so big, and evidently so heavy, that they make me think of the signs they put on cows in agricultural fairs I've been to in Maine-et-Loire. *You're right, Joe. These are some classy cows....* The dogs are excited by the crowd. They want to be set free to run or bite people. In the crush I almost get separated from my parents. Papa catches me by the sleeve *in extremis* as I'm being carried away by the current. Fortunately, we've been able to stay together, and now that we're being herded into a cattle car, the five of us, hand in hand, we feel almost relieved. We no longer risk being separated. Here's what's written on the heavy doors of the cattle car: "Horses end to end, 8; People, 40." We're a lot more than 40.

We've been locked inside for two hours, standing, squashed against each other, with no water or toilets. Suffocating in almost total darkness—there's only one small skylight for the whole car—we prick our ears to hear what's going on outside on the platform, but it's always the same thing: crying, shouts, dogs barking, French police officers yelling at their subordinates, and German officers drowning them out with their booming voices. Every once in a while, we can hear a blow on a shoulder, a head, a back. A prisoner cries out louder than the others—a sound that makes us freeze in fear. Petrified, we open our eyes wide. We want to find in another's face a sign that everything's going to be all right, for us at least, since no one's bothering with us anymore. We're locked up in darkness like animals, with no understanding of what's happening. And still with nothing to drink, nothing to eat, and no place to relieve ourselves with decency.

At noon, the train slowly begins to move. We're on our way, but no one knows where, so we have no idea how long the trip will take. Sometimes, a man stuck near the door peeks through a crack to try to guess where we are and where we're going.

"It looks like a place I know in Picardy. I think we're approaching Picardy. . . ."

"Everywhere looks the same, my friend."

"So we're going north?"

"I think it's probably east."

"Does anyone have a compass?"

"A compass. . . . Let's see. . . . A compass . . . oh, we forgot the compass!"

Some people still have the strength to smile. And then everyone is silent. For hours. We're moving slowly. Often the train stops, in the middle of the countryside. No one knows why or for how long. It's hot—surely more than 100 degrees. The train must have been out in the sun for hours before we climbed in. It feels like an oven. Every few minutes, one of the stronger men lifts a child up to the skylight so he can get a bit of air. I dream of my folding bed, my miserable bed that I had to open each night to go to sleep and close every morning at dawn—my child's bed whose springs squeaked at the slightest movement, with a mattress so thin that my hip went through. I imagine that I'm lying on it, between smooth, clean sheets as always. The room has its familiar silence. Rachel, asleep, makes little, irritating sighs. My father is snoring gently in the next room, and the wooden closet creaks every now and then. I always hated my folding bed, and now I have no idea when I'll be able to lie in it again. But one thing I know: I'm sure that I'll love it.

4 · Beaune-la-Rolande

In fact, the train was going southwest. The first stop is Pithiviers, where we wait a long time, straining our ears to hear. We can hear doors sliding open and footsteps on the platform as we await our turn. No one comes. In about eight hours we've gone only about sixty miles—a pathetically small distance that transported us a tiny bit closer to America and a tiny bit farther from Germany. That's as far as we're going today: Beaune-la-Rolande, for a two weeks' stay.

From the station, we have to walk several miles. We follow the rhythm imposed upon us, fear clutching at our hearts once again, with no idea where we're going. We tramp through the lifeless streets of the village, which are not only deserted but hostile: no lights in the windows, shutters closed. No sign of life, not even a stray cat. . . . Once we arrive at the camp, drained by our journey, exhausted from the heat, wiped out from five days in the Vél' d'Hiv, we collapse on the straw mattresses distributed to us. And we sleep, the men in one place and the women in another. I'm at the point where childhood meets adulthood. I haven't had my bar mitzvah yet, but I'm put with the men, which I find flattering.

There are several long barracks with a door at each end. Inside there are bedsteads on three levels, crushed one against the other. They assign me a place at the top.

The next morning we realize we won't be staying here for long. Those who can see the handwriting on the wall disabuse those who prefer not to see. From now on, the topic of conversation doesn't change from morning till night: The men walk around solemnly, with dark clothes and dark faces, repeating the same things:

"There have been others here before us: The mattresses are filthy. Some people wrote their names on the posts at the front of the dormitory or on tables outside."

"I found some letters in the straw behind my bed. . . ."

"They were imprisoned here, just like we are, and then they made room for us. But where do you think they went? They certainly didn't go back home!"

"If prisoners had been freed, we would have known in Paris. . . ."

Some of them hang onto hope that comes from somewhere I can't understand:

"Maybe they weren't set free, and maybe we won't be right away either, but they must have been taken to camps set up for Jews."

"It seems that we're being sent back to the countries we came from. That's why they told us to take warm clothes."

"Probably. Look at us, with our wives and our children! What could they possibly want to do with us? Pétain just wants to get us out of the way until things settle down."

"Pétain! You still trust Pétain?"

Just as at Père Fabri's bar, when the conversation heated up around a game of belote, Papa grabs me by the sleeve and pulls me away. "Come, let's go find your sisters."

"What about you, Papa? What do you think?"

He leans over me and winks knowingly: "Me? I think we're going to . . . *Pitchi Poï*!"

My father's referring to the Yiddish name for the imaginary village that's part of Polish popular culture. He's trying to tell me that he doesn't know where we're going but that he chooses to believe in a happy outcome to our adventure, as if it were a fairy tale. Amused, I join his game.

"To *Pitchi Poï*? Yay! And will we eat chewy bagels there? Gefilte fish? Chopped eggs?"

My father laughs. I know full well that nothing like that will be on our table wherever we're going, and he knows that I know. He laughs at my love for good food and at my happy nature, apparently intact after all we've just been through, which should really make us cry. I'm not afraid of *Pitchi Poï*. I'm not afraid of anything because he's here and I can feel his strong hand grasping mine.

I look at Mama, still beautiful despite her exhaustion, continuing to pray all day long. Among us are men and women full of hope. There may also be those who are trembling in fear, but I cover them with an opaque cloak, the same one as at the Vél' d'Hiv. I choose not to see them, not to hear their moaning. They can't touch me. The weather is beautiful in the camp, just like in Montmartre. I raise my nose to the sky as soon as the sun rises. I feel the wind in my hair, and the smell of a nearby gingerbread factory tickles my nostrils from time to time. I once ate some gingerbread, in the park. I can still remember. . . . It was good. Some day I'll have more, in *Pitchi Poï* or somewhere else.

Our days are always the same. At 7:00 a.m. we're served a thin, blackish liquid for "breakfast." We spend the morning—the oldest kids, too—doing all sorts of cleaning, which we continue in the afternoon after gobbling down our lunch—the end of a piece of bread and some kind of brew with a few weevily beans floating in it. At the end of the afternoon, we rush to get another bowl of broth, and as soon as night falls, it's lights out. Our fellow citizens might be angry with us for pillaging the wealth of France, but we're not costing the country much this summer. In fact, we're improving the economy: Everyone says that methodical searches are organized of people's belongings and persons, and that no one's going to leave here with the slightest object of value.

The other day I was told to empty the pail filled with the excrement from our barracks. I noticed it contained banknotes and jewels. I didn't say anything, and, obviously, I didn't take any. What would I do with them, anyway? I'll be leaving here just like everyone else, and I'll be forced to empty my pockets.

We're supposed to leave today. We were alerted yesterday over the loudspeaker. The Weismanns were named, along with hundreds of other families. Papa went to sign us up. It's five in the morning, the sun is barely up, and here we are in line waiting to be searched, in front of our barracks, deliberately emptied of internees, as we're called. There are only women, and I wonder why Mama asked me to accompany her. They're all bowing their heads in shame. I want to shout at them—they should be proud instead that they can still hold themselves together in spite of the hardships inflicted on them for these past weeks. Many have been separated from their husbands, either because they were arrested before their wives, when only men were rounded up, or because they couldn't find them in all the confusion at the Vél' d'Hiv.

I shouldn't say that they're ashamed, really; they're just terrified, and for good reason. The building was emptied of its bedsteads. On either side now are long tables with militiamen seated behind them, young guys dressed in black from head to toe, with berets on their heads and shoulder straps stretched diagonally across their chests. They're playing with their night-sticks, which they've set down in front of them. They have shifty, self-satisfied looks on their faces. They gloat over the humiliated women, who could be their mothers. Each time one approaches, they tap sharply on the wooden table, impatient: "Hand over your valuables, quickly. Jewelry, watches, money! Hurry up!"

I hear one scream, "What are you hiding in your bra?" His neighbor leans back in his chair and roars with laughter.

Soon it's our turn, but there's a fat woman ahead of us.

"Take off your clothes!"

She shakes her head no, crossing her hands over her breasts, her skin, her modesty. She cries silent tears, imploring. A militiaman walks forward and shakes her brutally. He pulls a bill out of her corset, throws it on the table, and strikes a violent blow to the back of his victim's neck. Mama stops breathing, and I clutch her, crying.

"It's nothing, Joseph . . . nothing."

It's not nothing. The woman is almost naked now, her garters hanging down her thick thighs. She's on the ground, and I find her to be fat and ugly. The sight of her frightens me as much as the blows of the man's boot. She's crying, screaming, begging him to stop kicking her, stop her humiliation and suffering, let her live! I'm ashamed to see her so distraught. And I'm ashamed of my shame. An immense malaise comes over me from this bad thought I'm having. I should be feeling only pity for this poor woman; instead I turn my eyes away. And what's next? I'm afraid for my mother! I couldn't bear to see her kicked this way. I couldn't tolerate it. Fortunately, we have nothing, and suddenly it's good never to have had anything. The little money that Mama was able to bring here has already been taken away by the police. They must have thought we'd bribe one of our guards to help us escape.

They don't make Mama undress, and we're able to leave the barracks by the door at the far end. We find ourselves standing in a large, open area, two additions to the small crowd that has already formed—and that's going to continue to grow and grow throughout the morning. The guards have separated us into two groups: men on one side and women and children, including my mother, my sisters, and me, on the other.

It's past noon. We haven't eaten since yesterday, and the sun is pounding on our heads. The heat conspires with our fate to make us even more miserable. And still we wait.

A policeman says, "You're going to be deported."

The sentence spreads through the dense, lethargic mass that we've become. The word is repeated, dissected, explained. "Deported? What does 'deported' mean?"

We're a herd of people, different from a herd of animals in only one respect: we're endowed with speech. In every other way, we're no better.

Germans have entered the camp. Since we arrived at Beaune-la-Rolande, it's the first time I've seen any. I have no reaction. I've ceased believing that they wish us more ill than the French police officers, since, from all appearances, the latter certainly don't wish us well. The soldiers look us up and down. I lower my head to avoid looking into their eyes. Bands of red fabric run the length of their legs. I'm impressed. Very sophisticated for soldiers' uniforms. Of course, they are the great, victorious army. . . .

How many hours have we been waiting out in the broiling sun on this sweltering summer day? I've lost all notion of time. The youngest kids aren't even crying anymore. Are they asleep?

They seem instead to be fainting from thirst and the heat. The women gather their last strength to show their children that there's still hope, that courage is keeping them going more than fear. But suddenly the Germans seem to be very angry. They want some explanations from the French police who brought us here. We future deportees aren't unduly worried: totally worn out by another terrible day, we're only solemn and resigned. Our fate has already been out of our hands for a long time. All we can do now is wait until others decide for us—and we have no illusions as to what's going to happen: We're going back into the cattle cars ("Horses end to end: 8; People: 40") to an unknown destination.

Not all the German soldiers are wearing pants with red bands. Only three or four, from what I can see. It's almost nighttime now. We still haven't had anything to eat or drink the entire day, and they're continuing their endless discussion at the entrance to the camp as if we don't exist. That's the reality: we don't exist for them, or at least not anymore. They were concerned with us only the time it took to gather us together and decide to deport us. The train is waiting in the Beaune-la-Rolande station, and as soon as the locomotive sets off, transporting us somewhere far away, they'll forget that we were here among them, as alive as they were, with beating hearts, eyes to see them, and brains to wonder at their cruelty.

Suddenly the officers separate and spread out in front of the women and children. Soldiers are standing across from us with their huge dogs. Their superiors give them orders that I can't understand. The calm that has existed up to now disappears in an instant. We had been mute, discouraged, dumbfounded, and totally exhausted. Now everyone begins to shout, and the tormentors' bellowing combines with the victims' screams.

A woman shrieks at the top of her lungs—but for whom? "The children! They're taking our children away from us!"

Instinctively, I try to move backward toward the center of the group, but it's impossible. There are too many of us, and we're all panicking uncontrollably, like an ant colony that someone has thrown a pebble into. A sharp cry emerges from the throats of mothers who have had a son or daughter torn away from them. Children struggle with all the strength left in their skinny limbs, whirling uselessly in the air as soldiers lift them up and throw them on the ground a few meters away.

The officers' eyes sweep over the families. Eeny meeny miny mo, they choose their victims randomly: "You, you, you!"

The children are snatched up and put off to one side. I don't know where to look. On every face I see a look of enormous distress that upsets me even more. On none is there any sign of encouragement, of consolation, the certainty that no, I'm not going to be selected, not me. The men try to fight back, too, with their bodies and their voices, but they receive blows in their ribs and on their heads. They're completely helpless. So, the adults are no longer in control of anything. I tremble like a leaf at the thought of being taken away from Mama. Where are my sisters? I look for them but can't find them. I guess that means that they're leaving, too. Like my father, I suppose. I grab onto Mama. She's my last defense against the hatred for Jews exploding around me, which I'm absorbing with ever-increasing awareness. She's everything to me. It's because of her that I'm still able to stand, that I'm still breathing, that soup still nourishes me, that the sun can still warm me. It's because of her that my heart continues to beat. It's for her that I want to grow up.

An officer approaches us. He wants to move quickly—to escape from the cries, to end this terrible moment, to lock the doors of this camp behind these furies and make these cursed Jews disappear. But I don't want to disappear. Actually, I do:

I want to disappear with Papa, Mama, Charlotte, and Rachel, but all together. I want to remove myself from their sight, become invisible if that will make them happy. I promise. I'll give up the parks of Montmartre for those of *Pitchi Poï*, even if they're full of pebbles. I won't play with Guéchou anymore, with Charret or Maurice; I won't watch the cute little schoolgirls walking with my sisters on their way home; I won't listen to the conversations in the bar in the Rue Cauchois. It doesn't matter to me. Everything is fine with me as long as I can stay with my mother.

The screaming is unbearable. I don't even hear it anymore. I don't think I can even really see all these distraught faces. These women throwing themselves on the ground, sobbing uncontrollably, in the depths of pain and despair—they're two yards from me, yet they suddenly seem far away. This horror... this horror is hell, if hell exists.

I'm a spectator at the events taking place all around me. I don't feel anything anymore, except the powerful, firm hand that grabs me by the arm and drags me away.

The night is as black as pitch now. I'm alone, on the dusty ground of the open area in the center of the camp. Next to me, another child is alone. Behind me, in front of me, as far as the eye can see in the light of the watchtowers, I see hundreds of lonely beings completely indifferent to others. We've cried so much that our tears have dried up. We've screamed so much that our voices are no longer audible. We've struggled so much that our bodies, drained of all strength, no longer respond. Snot is running from our noses. We don't even think to wipe it off on our sleeves. No one seems to care about us, mundane sackfuls of sorrow, inert and shapeless. Every once in a while, though, a woman in a white nurse's uniform comes to pick up a little one. He lets himself be led away just as a fruit allows itself to be picked. Where are they taking him? I don't really want to know. The torture inflicted on us by separating us so brutally from our parents has destroyed any impulse in us to be curious. I have no will to get up from where I'm lying, where nothing's going to happen anyway. Nevertheless, the moment comes when it seems like a good idea to go to sleep. I surprise myself by standing up, mechanically, and directing myself to barrack number 7. I climb up to my bed, unaware of the emptiness around me. And what do I do now? I call on the little voice in my head to rescue me, because it's all I have left: *Don't think, Joe. Don't think about anything. Sleep. Sleep while you can. Afterward, we'll see.*

It's morning, and I'm not happy with what I see. There's not one adult left in the camp, except our tormentors, who are guarding us with guns in their hands, as if three-year-old children could wake up as terrorists. A few nurses are giving out soup. The poor women are doing what they can, but there aren't enough of them for all these broken souls. They repeat to anyone who cares to listen, "Your parents have left to prepare the camp for your arrival. The police have promised that you'll be seeing them again soon."

Do they believe the police? They don't look that way. Not enough conviction in their voices, not enough sincerity in their eyes. Do they believe what they're saying? I don't. All you have to do is open your eyes to doubt their kind words. Some children are so young that they don't even know their last name, even less their address. A few of them were given labels, sewn onto their shirts or simply suspended on a piece of string. But the kids exchange them like trading cards. I saw a little boy named Rosine.... How can their parents ever find them again? They number in the thousands, and so do we.

"What are you doing there all alone in a corner? Come join the others. What's your name?"

"Joseph. Joseph Weismann." My eyes meet those of a grown-up for the first time since my mother closed hers in sorrow last night when they led her to the train. It's a kind, small woman hardly older than Charlotte, with her hair covered by a kind of wimple like the ones nuns wear. She looks overwhelmed, exhausted, but her heart is filled with hidden resources. She's already going to check on another boy.

Her work is pointless, her efforts pathetic. There are just too many of us. Hundreds, spread out in every corner of the camp, which seems empty to us now that our parents have been taken away. I can't even imagine them anymore, neither them nor my sisters, in that disgusting cattle car. My anger makes me nauseous. I'm mad at them for letting them round us up in Paris, and most of all for having left here without me. It doesn't matter that I know they had no choice, that they're no more responsible than I am for our separation: my anger is too painful. I'm enraged by this horrible injustice. If looks could kill, that guard over there would fall to the ground. Maybe he has a son, a boy my age, dark like me, or daughters who resemble my sisters. They would find themselves alone like me, and this policeman, this monster, would get just what he deserves. I scan the camp from one end to the other. I fire at anyone in uniform. Bang bang bang! They drop like flies, the bastards.

We're a sorry sight. The youngest ones are walking around with shit on their underwear, or even naked. The oldest have faces black with a mixture of dust and tears. Our mothers aren't here to tell us to go wash ourselves, and the idea doesn't occur to us on our own. Siblings find one another. You can see the older ones holding their little brothers' hands. The little ones clasp them tightly with the energy of despair. I have no one left, and I think about my sisters. I want to press them against me. I'd try to reassure them by my presence as much as they'd comfort me for being separated from our parents.... But there's only one Weismann left in the camp of Beaune-la-Rolande: me.

Many children lean listlessly against a fence. In the middle of a passageway, a little girl four years old at most has simply lain down on the ground, indifferent to the bodies brushing against her, to the feet bumping into her by accident. Our hearts broken, we've been abandoned, destroyed physically and emotionally. I look at us all, and I wonder why this was done to us. I look at myself, Joseph Weismann, eleven years old, Parisian and Jewish, miserable but lucid at the same time. Why was this done to us?

The most astonishing thing is that life is reasserting itself. Little by little, groups are forming. Pebbles are becoming jacks. A stick traces squares for hopscotch.

As for me, I've already made up my mind. I'm getting the hell out of here.

5 · Escape

"Hey, you! Wanna escape?"

The boy shrugs his shoulders. I turn to his neighbor.

"What about you? You want to come with me?"

The two of them think I'm completely nuts. "What's the matter with you? We're going to be with our parents in ten days. Why would you want to leave?"

I go on my way, searching for the ideal escape partner. Every time I notice a boy who looks bigger and stronger than me, I repeat my question.

"I'm getting outta here. Wanna come?"

I finally find one who smiles as soon as I tell him my idea. But it doesn't last long: "I can't. I have a hernia."

"So what? No problem—bring it with you!"

He bursts out laughing. "Don't make me laugh. It makes it hurt even more."

I walk away before he realizes how stupid I am: I thought a hernia was a musical instrument.

I avoid groups, whenever I find several guys ready to share in my adventure: I know that if there are only two of us, we'll succeed, but with three or more, it'll be easy to notice us. I keep a low profile and crouch down every time I see a bigger, stronger boy than me. There's no lack of them. . . . Some hesitate, but never for long. The idea flits about in their shaved heads—shaved because of lice—and the answer pops out like a receipt from a cash register: "Impossible."

I don't get discouraged. I ask them tirelessly, one by one. Most of them just shake their heads to let me know that there's no need to go on. Some are more curious: "And how do you intend to go about this?"

"Don't worry. I have a plan!"

For the moment, I'm still lying to a certain extent. If I were perfectly honest, I'd say that I have a goal in mind: to get out of this place alive with an accomplice as brawny as the superheroes in my favorite comic strips. In unity there is strength. Before the war, I often heard grown-ups repeat this sentence in the café in the Rue Cauchois. They read the papers, commented on the news, and spoke about starting a revolution, all of them together. Too bad they didn't decide to do this at the Vél' d'Hiv or even here. Besides, I only half believe their motto: From what I can see, unity can divide as well. It's impossible to get everyone to agree. But that's not important: I'm going to have my own little revolution. It won't make any noise, and it will occur completely unnoticed, but it will save us. There will be two of us. We'll tell the police and the Krauts to go screw themselves. (Quietly, as soon as we're out in the countryside.) They won't hear us? Just as well! The later they come running after us, the better off we'll be.

Evening comes. Time for our soup. It tastes more like tea than a real bouillon. . . . If we're lucky, a few beans will be floating on top. I'm sure not going to gain any weight from this! I haven't yet found my accomplice—absolutely essential, I'm convinced, for the simple reason that I'm too thin and weak to get through the wall of barbed wire surrounding us by myself.

Apparently, the wires are twisted around one another and held together by other wires, the whole thing several meters high. An inextricable lattice. Not to worry: I'm sure I can get through it as long as I have two other hands to help me.

The next morning, bingo! Two boys I had spoken to the night before approach me.

"Did you change your mind?"

"Not us. We want to wait to see our parents again. But you see the boy over there leaning on the door of the barracks? We spoke to him, and he said that he was planning to escape, too."

"Thanks, guys. I'm gonna go talk to him. Not a word of this to anyone, OK?"

"Not a word. We promise."

It's more than I could have hoped for. From where I'm standing, I take a good look at my potential partner. The candidate isn't much taller than me, but his shoulders are twice as broad. He's alone. The fact that he isn't talkative is a plus. I puff out my chest and approach him. I don't want him to think I'm too skinny to carry this off.

"Hi. The two guys over there told me that you're planning to get out of here."

"Absolutely. You, too?"

"Whenever you're ready. What's your name?"

"Joseph Koganovitch. My friends call me Joe." He stretches his hand, like a man.

"A pleasure, Joe. My name's Joseph. I think I'll use the whole thing. So . . . are you ready, Joe?"

Without hesitating, we head for the barbed wire and walk along it as though we're seeing it for the first time. But there are guards posted, observing us from the watchtowers. We both have the same idea at the same time: "The food shed!"

The food shed is the building closest to the barbed wire fence. If we're able to go around and slip in behind it, we have a chance of not being seen from the two watchtowers at the entrance to the camp. Of course, there are the other two, on each side. . . . We sneak over without being noticed. A piece of a board lying there might be useful. We pick it up and start to lean it against the wall in the hope of passing over the top. Curious kids begin to watch us. Then more . . . and more. No use complaining to them that they're putting us in danger of getting caught: Distractions are very rare here, and the show we're putting on already seems to have them frozen in place. Of course, it doesn't take long for the guards to arrive, blowing their whistles loudly. We scatter among the barracks like sparrows. I lose Joe in the mêlée, but we'll catch up with each other later.

But what if this plan is impossible? I need to remotivate myself. The little voice in my head tells me to get a grip before trying again. I crouch in a corner and enter into one of those internal dialogues that always produce valuable advice:

Really, Joseph, what got into your head? Why would you think about escaping from here? You don't even have anywhere to go! And what if you did? Don't you want to see your parents again?

Of course, that's all I think about.

So why leave? The police, the nurses, even the other kids in the camp told you: you'll see them in two weeks.

Um . . . I, uh . . . don't believe that.

Why not? What doubts could you possibly have?

I don't really know. I think I'm going to see them again some day, but not by getting in a train like the one that took them away the day before yesterday.

So at least that is decided. My instinct, or something else, leads me to think that I should no longer listen to those who say. . . . Until last Thursday, July 16, I would never have doubted the word of an adult. I swallowed what I was told without even thinking about the reasoning behind it. The good manners that my parents had inculcated in me had done their work: I never argued with a grown-up, and if I sometimes had my own ideas, I kept them to myself. But all that's over. They've lied too much. They've behaved badly. My parents listened to them, they followed their instructions, and where did that get them? Yes, where . . . I'd really like to know. I'll never trust anyone but myself ever again. And this Joe, maybe, because he's eleven years old and is prepared to risk everything to get out of here.

———

Joe met up with me while I was enjoying my breakfast, a tasty blackish liquid served in a metal cup with a deliciously . . . metallic taste. Nurses had handed out milk to the youngest children. It's hard to look at them—miserable, dirty, lost. Half crazy since they were torn away from their parents. All night long I can hear them moaning and crying, calling their mothers. They wake one another up, and pretty soon they're all sobbing. It never ends. Fortunately, some of them have older sisters or brothers to comfort them. I'm all alone now. There's nothing to keep me here.

"Joe, I've been thinking. We went about things like jerks yesterday."

"You're right, Joseph. We gotta get organized. And we need to think about what we're going to do once we get out of here. Do you have any money?"

"No, but I think I know where I can find some. . . ."

My new friend acts totally disgusted when he sees me plunge my arm up to the elbow in the excrement, and he's stunned when I happily take out a few pieces of black, wet paper: the banknotes I had noticed during my chores.

"Joseph, you're a strange guy. . . ."

I giggle in silence. We're not here for a laugh. This escape is nothing like finding your way out of the Parc Monceau in Paris. I'm completely aware of the danger we're in. The guards are armed. We risk a whole lot more than a few whacks on the calves with a switch. If they capture us with the money, it won't be so bad. And anyway, if they were dumb enough not to realize that the prisoners threw their cash in the latrines so they couldn't have it, I don't see why they'd bother to search us. I shake my treasure under Joe's nose, and he gets splashed a little.

"You know what that is?"

"Yep. Shit."

"Shit can be washed off. And underneath you'll see that there are several nice banknotes."

Joe serves as lookout while I rinse our booty. The harvest was good: three new 100-franc bills. In this heat, they'll be dry in less than an hour. Now we just have to put the finishing touches on our plan.

We begin a methodical exploration of the camp. Only the entrance gate isn't protected by tight rows of barbed wire, but it immediately appears impassable to us. It's guarded by several teams of *gendarmes*, inside and out. So we'll have to deal with the barbed wire, no matter how sharp and thick it is. Going over the top of it is out of the question: First of all, it's too high—more than two yards from the looks of it. And it seems to extend over a long distance, so we could be seen too easily. We consider digging, but the soil, dried up by the summer heat, is too hard. One last option presents itself to us, the one that will work: separate the metal wires to create a passage.

The camp is shaped like a rectangle, and there's a watchtower at each corner. At night, the police sweep the open area and the edges with spotlights, ready to fire at anything that moves. We might as well try to escape in the daytime.

"We need to choose the moment when there's the most activity," Joe suggests.

Together we exclaim, "Lunchtime!"

At noon, everyone assembles in front of the food shed for the only meal of the day. Of course, no one wants to run the risk of missing lunch, so it's there that all the guards' eyes are focused while the food is being given out—about two hours in total.

Joe is worried. "The barbed wire is really thick. . . . We're gonna be skinned alive."

"You're right, but we don't have any choice. We're going to have to equip ourselves. . . . Do you know where to find some sturdy clothes?"

He knows. The clothes left behind by everyone who's passed through the camp have all been put in one of the barracks. We sneak inside unnoticed. Sweaters, pants, and shirts are piled up on the bedsteads, with no regard for size or shape. No problem—we do the sorting ourselves. . . . Toward the end of the morning, with the August sun shooting out its hottest rays, here we are, dressed for wintertime: two pairs of underwear, two pairs of pants, two shirts, and a thick wool beret on our shaved heads, everything in the darkest colors we can find, brown and dark green. We stay far from the others and pretend to be sleeping, leaning against the wall of one of the barracks the way so many other kids do. . . .

I imagine that thoughts like mine are racing through Joe's head. It's been two days since our parents were taken away. We haven't even taken the time to tell each other about our lives. All I know about him is that he lives in the twentieth arrondissement and that he has no brothers or sisters. We adopted each other spontaneously because we share the same taste for freedom, and also maybe a certain clearheadedness. We don't formulate a plan—we're barely conscious of what we're about to do, but we sense that we have to do it. Something deep inside of us sets off an alarm: We have to get out of here; it's a question of life or death.

There are no smiles on our faces at the thought of our flight. On the contrary, we're serious, worried, and filled with emotion. We look at the other children. Some of them aren't even three years old, and few are as old as we are. Many are sick from what they've been eating for weeks, and perhaps even more from the privation they've endured for years now. Some play, oblivious. The rage to live that compels Joe and me to want to escape drives them only to go running through the dust of the camp as they wait to rush into their parents' arms. Hope or some kind of reckless unawareness keeps them going, I don't know. Just like Joe and me in the end, except we're going in another direction. They're all like the two of us: the same yellow star sewn on their chests, the same imprisonment, the same nightmares, the same hunger gnawing at their stomachs—and, in all our hearts, the same boundless love for our fathers and mothers. The lunch bell rings at the other end of the camp. We watch the children pop out of every corner to go get their piece of bread.

The two of us take off.

—⁓—

Joe goes first. Flat on his stomach, nose in the dust, he begins to separate the barbed wire to create a kind of tunnel through it on the ground. But it takes him many minutes to disentangle even one inch because the wires are so tightly enmeshed. It's nothing like the open wire fences surrounding fields of cows! The wall before us seems to be made of an impossible tangle of rolls of metal wire. I heard from the grown-ups, when they were still here, that the camp was originally built to keep German soldiers prisoner. If the security fence around the camp was judged sufficient for solid, well-nourished soldiers, it's reasonable to conclude that two skinny runts like Joe and me have no chance of escape. Only we're absolutely not reasonable.

Fortunately, Joe is big. . . . After an hour of effort and perseverance, he's succeeded in creating a passage just wide enough for someone his size, and now that it's long enough, I slide in behind him. We advance at the pace of a sickly snail through the mass of metallic brambles so thick that the sunlight can barely penetrate it, but we're still moving forward. And we have plenty of time: it's not like in school. No one's taking attendance, and no one's waiting for us. And if we're not there tonight in our dormitory for lights out, no one's going to notice. Even if a guard making his rounds passes by the hole we made in the barbed wire, he'll have to bend down to see it. I wouldn't say we were calm, but our adventure seems to be off to a pretty good start.

Joe is breathing hard in front of me. My nose is on his heels. There's no real reason to be this close except to encourage him. All of his precautions are in vain: protecting his hands with the sleeves of his shirt to separate the wires one by one, he still tears up his fingers. "Ow! These damned things really hurt!"

"Joe, be quiet! You're going to attract attention!"

"Easy for you to say. I'm bleeding everywhere."

"It's all right. It's all right. We're moving ahead."

"Well, I can't keep doing this. It's your turn."

There's one problem: the passageway he's made isn't wide enough for us to pass each other, even though I've enlarged it a little. We crawl backward toward the camp. I get out, Joe follows me, and I creep back into the tunnel, with Joe right behind me. We hold our breath for a few seconds. Nothing happens. There's still the same noise, the same sobs, the same shouts of children who have lost control of themselves. No one saw us, no gendarme on his rounds, no policeman from his watchtower, probably because of the thickness of the barbed wire.

My index fingers and thumbs form pliers precise enough to grab hold of the wires and separate them one by one. I'm panting and cursing like my friend before me, but soon I clear a four-inch-long passage wide enough for our shoulders. I suddenly move my head, and my beret gets stuck on the barbs. Is it lice, fleas, scabies, or scratches from the wires? I'm not sure what's itching. Besides, pretty soon I don't feel anything. Neither the blood flowing down my hands, elbows, and neck nor the skin being peeled off my knees from rubbing against the ground. I hear Joe breathing behind me, but we don't speak. We have no need to urge each other on. And we have to conserve our strength, because this is a long—a very long—procedure. How long has it been since we started to make our way through this mass of barbed wire? It seems like hours.

In fact, it has been hours, but we're unaware. Once again, we've lost the notion of time. We have only one idea in our minds: pass under this wall of metal, make it out, and stand in the fresh air of freedom. We have no choice: it's not hard to imagine what would happen to us if we were to go back. We have no knowledge that elsewhere members of the Resistance are joining forces and singing "Freedom guides our footsteps." But it's the idea of this same freedom that helps us to endure our painful crawl. We're exhausted, but in no way discouraged, firmly convinced that we're going to succeed.

We're right. After many hours, I catch a glimpse of brighter light. I redouble my effort. Anesthetized by the pain, my hands no longer feel anything. I pick up the pace, helped by luck: the network of metal wires is a little less dense near the outside of the enclosure. Suddenly, right in front of me, I see a hole about eight inches in diameter already formed in the wires. Could some villager secretly have tried to create a passage into the camp to see what was going on there? Or to help prisoners escape? Who knows? In any case, he didn't finish the job. Joe

and I, on the other hand, have almost completed our work.
With my last remaining strength, I create a tunnel to the hole
I just discovered. I take off my beret, and, in a gesture of rage,
I throw it outside.

"Joe, my beret is free!"

"Dickhead! I don't believe it! You still need it!"

"I don't care. Maybe I'm not out yet, but my beret is, and I'm
planning to join it!"

I hear my friend grumbling behind me. "What a moron! He's
going to cut his head open at the last minute. . . . Whatever got
into me to try this with such a halfwit?"

"Joe, keep your insults to yourself. We made it!"

"We made it? I don't believe it."

"It's true, I swear."

"What do you see?"

There's an open space. We're going to have to run a little to
reach the trees. I'd say . . . about twenty yards. Are your legs
still working?"

"Don't worry—they're fine. . . . Get a move on, and wave to
me when you're there, OK?"

"OK!"

I pick up my beret and launch myself like a rocket. My shoes
race forward, and my little sparrow's feet follow them as best
they can. I squeeze my fists with all my remaining strength.
It's the most beautiful run of my life—I fly, I slide, I skid, and
finally I throw myself into the ditch! I feel like shouting with
joy, like dancing, like swinging from the branches like a mon-
key. In a fraction of second, however, the little voice in my head
brings me back to reality: *Calm down, Joseph, calm down. You're
only halfway there. There's still Joe. . . .*

No chance that I'll forget him. I'm fully aware of the fact
that I couldn't have succeeded without him. This little, slightly
chubby guy, hardly any heftier than me really, has earned his

freedom as much as I have. I lie flat on my stomach in the grass and study the space separating us. About as long as a school yard. If a gendarme, up in his watchtower, catches sight of Joe, it's all over. I can see only shapes up there: I can't make out which way the guards are facing. We'll have to take our chances. Joe is watching me, on the lookout for the slightest sign. I wave him over.

He springs up like a goat. In less time than it takes to tell about it, he's already on the ground next to me, sweating, panting, in really bad shape but alive and free! No troubling sounds come from the camp. The gendarmes didn't see us, or they didn't want to see us—we don't care which. Joe catches his breath and extends his hand.

"We did it, Joseph! We did it!"

"We did it, but you're a mess!"

He bursts out laughing. "Look who's talking!"

What time must it be? We started to inch our way through the barbed wire when the lunch bell sounded. Now the sun is much lower in the sky, and it's not as hot. It must be late in the afternoon. So it took us at least five hours to make our way through that briar patch of metal. How many yards did we go? Fifteen, I'm sure, maybe more.

"Joseph, we can't hang around here too long."

"I know. But I'm exhausted."

"Come, let's get away from here."

—◦◦◦—

From the ditch where we're lying, we can see a road, about 100 yards away. The trees in this thicket should be able to hide us until we can reach it. We decide to take a chance and move closer. Hardly have we set foot on the road when we hear footsteps behind us. The gendarmes have better shoes than ours—which is good, because that's how we can tell they're approaching. We throw ourselves back in the ditch, holding our breath until we can't see the two men anymore—and they can't see us.... They're making their rounds. Soon they'll summarize their findings to their superior: nothing to report! We heave a half sigh of relief: we suspect that the fright we experienced isn't the last of its kind.

"Joe, do you know where to go?"

"Before the war, I spent a vacation in a village nearby, with some really nice people. I'm sure they'll take us in."

"Are they Jewish?"

"Um . . . no, why?"

"Let's drop it. You know where they live? I mean . . . do you know how to get there from here?"

"I remember the name of the village, Lorris. If we walk up this road, we'll come to a crossroads with signs."

"This village—is it far?"

"I have no idea."

I don't dare tell him that maybe this isn't a good idea. That there's no guarantee we can trust these people even if he spent time with them several years ago. One word—and only one—has been echoing in my scratched-up head since we escaped from the camp: freedom. Before being rounded up in the Vél' d'Hiv and sent to Beaune-la-Rolande, it never even occurred to me that someone would want to take it away from me. I believed that, since I was born in France, I was automatically French. I just discovered that I'm Jewish first, like it or not.

We throw away our outer layer of clothes. The ones underneath are almost as torn up. We rip off the yellow stars, and the holes that are left in the fabric of our shredded garments are almost invisible. From now on, we're two hunted animals. And, like an animal, I follow only my instincts. They say to me: *Hide, you're not welcome here. Your parents are undesirables in France. They've already been sent away. They were barely tolerated*

*for a few years. You inherited your mother's pretty brown curls and
your father's gray-green eyes. But from their union, from both your
parents together, you inherited being Jewish. You're only the son of
a couple of poor Polish immigrants who will never be naturalized
French. They're not from here, so you're not, either.*

And neither is Joe. But what can we do, alone in the middle
of a forest with nothing to eat or drink?

"Listen, Joe. Soon it will be night, and we risk meeting up
with other gendarmes or even farmers. You see that forest over
there? The best thing to do is to spend the night there. With a
little luck, we'll find some blackberries to eat. And then we'll
decide what to do."

He follows me. We run into the trees, deep into the woods,
walking beside a path. As it gets darker and darker, we feel all
the fatigue of the past few weeks weighing on us. All the ten-
sion we contained while we were separating the barbed wires,
trembling at the thought of being caught, finally releases itself.
We're not even hungry, thirsty, or afraid. We don't feel or per-
ceive anything. Tall oak trees, imperturbable, tower over our
poor heads. We curl up in a cradle of tree roots and sink into a
dreamless sleep.

It's no small thing for a child from Montmartre to spend the
night under the stars. On summer evenings, when we open the
windows of our apartment, all we hear is the sounds of the city.
They sound like the daytime ones, only softer, plus the kids
are sleeping. At dawn, when I open my eyes, I don't recognize
anything. It takes me a few seconds to understand where I am
and who this boy lying next to me is. I prick my ears. The forest
has its own life at night, and I discover that it's terribly noisy. It
creaks, squeals, and cracks all over the place. There's something
disturbing in this fairy-tale atmosphere, but I already feel far

less distressed than in the camp, where the children cried in their sleep, never able to rest. I think about my father. I talk to him in secret while Joe is still asleep.

"Do you remember, Papa? How old was I? Maybe about seven. I left the house. Yes, I left all by myself. I was really angry. I hated the whole world that day—me most of all, or maybe Mama, I'm not sure. Besides, I don't even know what got me into such a state. I remember only the feeling of injustice stirring inside me. We had had an argument, and we had shouted. I had even cried, but I didn't get anywhere. So I slammed the door in a rage. In my mind, it was all over! I was never again going to set foot in that room where no one understood me. No, Papa—don't put words in my mouth. That room where no one understood me, not where I was treated so badly. . . . It doesn't matter. There I was outside, furious. I walked and walked. All the anger that was crushing my chest and preventing me from breathing had descended to my legs, and I was convinced that I could walk around the entire earth without stopping. I started with the neighborhood, but I couldn't go fast enough, and that made me even angrier. Too many people in the street, too many kids, too many vegetable sellers.

"I headed toward the Parc Monceau. There, I thought to myself, I'll find the space I need. It's a fancy neighborhood—broad avenues, buildings with six or seven floors, beautiful façades with unbelievable sculptures. Rich people come to the park in the afternoon with huge snacks—so huge that they can't finish them all, so they share. They'll share a little bit with me, if they wish—and if they don't want to right away, I'll talk to them and make them laugh. I'll win them over, and they'll give in. And if they don't give in, I'll fight with them. I'm not afraid to get into a fight. I need to save some of the fury raging through my legs so it can move to my hands.

"I thought I was big, Papa. I thought I was big and strong, and I wasn't afraid of anything. But tonight, here, under my tree, I suddenly feel very small. . . .

"Do you remember, Papa? You found me on the Boulevard des Batignolles. I was at a Wallace fountain getting ready to quench my thirst. I had grabbed the metal cup hanging from a chain and had already begun to bring it to my lips when I felt your hand on my shoulder. And then I heard your voice, soft, peaceful, calm: 'Don't drink from there, Joseph. You'll get sick. All the bums drink from that same cup. . . .'

"I had left you forever, but you spread the warm, reassuring, protective blanket of your love over me again. All my anger slipped away at once. We walked back home hand in hand. I felt a little ridiculous surrendering so easily, but I had also won a victory. I had won a walk with you, side by side, through the streets of Paris. That was something that didn't happen very often.

"Will I ever see you again, Papa? Will I be able to tell you what Joe and I just did? Will you believe me? I'm not sure I do myself."

———

"I'm starving. I'll even eat acorns, I'm so hungry."

"What if we decided to try to find a piece of bread instead?"

"Joseph, let me remind you that we don't have any rationing tickets."

"We have something even better, remember? Three 100-franc bills, nice and warm inside my sock!"

It's morning now. We walk along beside the path that crosses the woods, at a prudent distance, though: No one can take a carefree walk nowadays, but we two have to worry about the gendarmes, and, who knows, maybe even the Germans. Having reached the edge of the forest, we spot a small village a few hundred yards in front of us. We charge straight ahead. A sign tells us the name of the village: Boiscommun. From all appearances, the inhabitants are lacking in hospitality for their German occupiers, or else they've all left. It's already broad daylight, but all the doors and windows are shut tight. Even the shutters seem hermetically sealed. But it appears that luck is smiling on us: a bakery just raised its curtain. We rush in and come back out with our hands full of brioches and rolls. The money we paid with didn't surprise the salesgirl any more than our torn-up clothes and filthy faces.

On the other hand, a band of kids we encounter as we leave Boiscommun seems a little too interested in us. There are five or six of them, about our age judging from appearances, and they start to chase us. We pick up the pace, and they begin to throw stones at us! Joe urges me to run faster, but I think we should confront them before things take a bad turn and they alert the entire surrounding area. I turn around and walk toward them.

"Hi. What do you want?"

My composure, along with my confident smile, disarms them.

"Uh . . . nothing."

"Well, you're following us. . . . Are you looking for some friends? My name's Joseph, and my friend here is named Joe."

"Are you gypsies?"

This time I don't have to force a smile. They may be old enough to be outside on their own, but these kids are hardly better dressed than we are, and in any case no cleaner! Instinctively, I sense that it would be in my interest to take advantage of being Parisian. With a bit of disdain, I decide I can impress these little hicks who are questioning us so distrustfully. . . .

"Where're the two of you from?"

"We just got here from Paris. Our parents sent us here on vacation. You see, there are things in the sky everywhere right now."

"Things in the sky? What're you talkin' about?"

"Planes, of course, bombardments!"

Their eyes open wide. If I'm convincing enough, they'll take us for heroes.

"Almost every night the sirens sound all over the city."

I imitate the noise, my hands around my mouth like a funnel, and I encourage Joe to do the same. The kids eat up every word.

"As soon as we hear them, we run down to our basements, unless we're sick and tired of that."

"Ain't you afraid?"

"Bah ... it's mostly our moms who are scared. ... Sometimes we sit by the window and watch the planes drop bombs around the neighborhood."

Joe catches on fast. His arms out to the side, he leans one way, then another, imitating the bombardiers.

"Tatatatatata! Brrooooom!"

"So you can understand, since there's so much noise and we can't sleep, our parents thought we'd be better off here."

They all agree, their mouths hanging open.

"We're going that way. Wanna come with us?"

Joe gives me a dirty look. He's in a hurry to be rid of them. I, on the contrary, think they'll make rather reassuring escorts. If we meet up with any gendarmes, assuming anyone has taken note of our escape from Beaune-la-Rolande, they won't think that we're hiding among the boys of the neighboring village. In any case, they quickly tire of the walk and decide to go back. We separate on very good terms.

"See you around!"

I wonder what they're going to tell their parents at dinner tonight. . . .

Once Joe and I have regained our composure, we laugh at our little adventure. But we're aware that it could have ended up in a much more dramatic fashion. A sign says that Lorris, the county seat, is only six miles away. That's where we need to go to find Joe's friends. With full stomachs, but not fully rested from the previous day's efforts, we decide to hide by the side of the road until the next day so no one else sees us. We'll start on our way again at dawn, while it's still half dark, when the village children—and the gendarmes—aren't snooping around.

――――

After our second night under the stars, we snake our way through the countryside in order to avoid the busiest roads— even the paths. We walk all day, rarely stopping, often afraid we're lost. Once we're close to Lorris, Joe finds the road to his friends' house as if he'd been there just the day before. It's a small farm, a little bit outside the village, in a minuscule group of houses. The mother and son are alone. They recognize Joe and usher us inside fearfully.

"Do you know that everyone in the area is looking for you? Sit down. I'll serve you some soup, and then you better get out of here!"

I can't believe it. This woman—this mother—who knows Joe for years is ready to throw us out just as night is falling! We tell her about everything, from the Vélodrome d'Hiver to the train that took our parents away. She knows that we're in danger of being picked up at any moment, but she doesn't want to do anything to help us. She probably can't imagine the conditions in the camp at Beaune. Maybe she believes that our parents are waiting for us in a comfortable place set up for us somewhere beyond the French border. Maybe she's not thinking about any-thing: she's afraid only for her own safety and that of her son. It's even likely that she just doesn't want any trouble. What difference does it make? We've just spent two cold nights out in the open, we've walked hours and hours today, we're in an area that we're not familiar with, the gendarmes are looking for us, and she doesn't want to help us.

Once again, without my parents, I feel terribly alone, and I have the feeling that this is the way it's going to be from now on. Before he led me to these people's house, I asked Joe if we could trust them. He was sure we could. Of course, they serve us a big bowl of soup like nothing we've had for weeks. They help us to get cleaned up and even give us each a clean shirt. But all this seems pathetic in the face of everything we need so desperately since our escape: a bed, a roof, a feeling of safety for one night. Just one night. . . .

We're back outside, shoulders bent, discouraged for the first time since we made it out of the camp. We don't want to sleep in a ditch or under a tree again. No more swaggering. We're children, after all. Only children. We need a bed, the protection of a kindly adult, some time to rest. Is that too much to hope for? Apparently it is. No one's home at the first door we knock on. At the second, we're greeted by an embarrassed refusal. At the third, we're met with grumbling and sent on our way. At the fourth, no one even bothers opening the door, although light is filtering through the shutters.

Finally, a woman lets us in. In a few words, we explain our situation: we're alone, we have no more families, we're tired. All we want is to lie down for a few hours, and we promise to leave the next morning. We obviously don't say that we're Jewish, and we show off our best manners. Our hostess doesn't smile, but she doesn't seem hostile, either. However, when we finish talking, she simply puts on a jacket, takes each of us by the hand, and leads us outside.

"Come, children. I know who can take care of you."

We understand what she's up to too late: we're on our way to the police station. Joe and I look at each other in despair. It's all over. We did it all for nothing. In an hour, maybe—at the latest tomorrow morning—we'll be taken back to the camp of Beaune-la-Rolande. We'll be locked up like dogs again, starved again, offered up to the whims of the Germans, to whom we'll soon be handed over just like our parents.

One of the two uniformed men seems delighted at our arrival. "Thank you, Madame, you did the right thing to bring them here! Let's go, boys. We don't have a cell, but there's a place for you over here. It's called the tramps' hole...."

He takes us by the arm and drags us to the little room. Once he's alone with us, he says to us, gently, "I understand your situation. Rest a little, and tomorrow the door will be open. There's a bus every morning for the Montargis station. From there, you can go to Paris...."

I fall into Joe's arms, and we cry for all we're worth. We don't believe this guy. He's as bad as the old witch who brought us here. We're doomed for sure. Doesn't this part of France have one adult who doesn't hate Jews? Exhausted, we fall asleep, our cheeks still wet with tears. After a few hours' sleep, I open my eyes and sit up. The little voice in my head speaks to me, in a light, conspiratorial tone:

Go ahead, Joseph. Take a look. What can you lose?

Listen, I know the damned door is locked.

You don't know anything of the kind. You didn't even try to open it.

I stand up almost in spite of myself. I drag myself to the bars and, believe it or not, the door moves. I push it a little more, still incredulous. I expect the gendarmes to pop out with their nightsticks raised. But the courtyard is empty.... I wake up Joe, who sits up with a start. We jump for joy and rush out of this hole! The air feels good. . . . But there's no time to waste. We have to locate the stop for the bus to Montargis.

We find it quickly, but we approach it trembling. The gendarmes are there, too. It looks as though they've been waiting for us. It's the same two from yesterday! The four of us wait patiently until the bus arrives. It finally appears and stops right in front of us. The driver announces to the men in uniform, "The bus is full. I can't take any more passengers."

"In that case, make two get out, and let these children in. They must take the first train to Paris."

"I'm telling you it's full. All they can do is wait for the next one this afternoon."

"And I'm telling you that they have to get in now. . . ."

I find a seat near the front, and Joe settles in a few yards behind me. We make ourselves as small as possible, aware that our luck could change at any moment. We're not out of the woods yet, but these two men, at least, have done what they could to get us closer to our goal.

Climbing into the bus, I take a good look at them, my eyes filled with tears of gratitude.

But I'm too afraid of the driver and the other passengers to say anything. Not even a little thank you. I hope they understand.

6 · Parisian Wanderings

"Which way are you going?"

"I have relatives in Ménilmontant. Maybe they'll take me in. And you?"

"No idea. I've got nobody."

"Come with me!"

"No, I'd rather go back to my house. Remember? Joseph Weismann, 54 Rue des Abbesses. Will we see each other again?"

"I hope so. Good luck whatever happens."

In the bus, and later in the train, we were trembling with fear that someone would ask to see our papers, which, obviously, we don't have. Now we're outside the Gare d'Austerlitz, the same station we left from on July 20, more than three weeks ago. And we're still trembling. It's not the forest we have to deal with, or a village of aggressive kids, but something even worse: at any moment we can meet up with the police or German soldiers armed to the teeth. What will happen if they stop us, if they ask us what we're doing in the street, running as though the Devil himself is hot on our heels? What will I do if they ask me my name?

I watch Joe head toward the Bastille. As for me, I make my way along the river in the opposite direction—straight north. Soon I'm on the Île de la Cité. I bypass the Halles, take the Boulevard de Sébastopol, and I can already see Sacré-Coeur. I walk straight toward it, never taking my eyes off it, as if it were life's ultimate goal, a warm, protective home. I know it's an illusion—no one's waiting for me. Nevertheless, I have only one thing in mind: make it back, all the way to the door of my apartment. I want to touch it, come full circle, return to my starting point and begin all over again.

Before the roundup, I walked through that door so often, almost always in a joyful mood. If someone gives me a notebook, I'll take the time do the math: count the number of times I went out, book bag on my back, on my way to school on the Rue Lepic. I'll add the Thursdays, Sundays, and vacation days, and then I'll find the total for the whole year. Next I'll multiply by eleven for all the years I lived there completely carefree. . . . I'll be able to figure out how many Saturdays I went through that door to go to the synagogue—of course, with a certain amount of complaining. . . .

———

I cross the threshold of 54 Rue des Abbesses. Today the little flower lady isn't there. Otherwise, nothing has changed. The concierge's door is closed. I don't expect to see her curtain move: Madame Auger isn't a busybody. She doesn't watch the comings and goings of the tenants except at night. I walk quickly through the front building, then the courtyard. I start up the stairs, holding my breath. I climb up one floor, then another, slowly, until I get to the fifth. Once I'm in front of the door of my apartment, I touch the wood with the palm of my hand. The wax seals that the policemen attached are still in place, untouched. I hadn't seen what kind of seal they used: a swastika. A couple of inches from this crude design, low enough for a five-year-old to touch, is the *mezuzah* that Mama never forgot to graze with her fingertips as she left the apartment, placing her home under the protection of God. On July 16, did she have time? I don't remember. Our departure is already hazy in my memory.

I don't linger to whine on the landing. I know it won't do any good. Besides, the tears don't come. I do feel something heavy in my chest, a weight pressing down on me, making it hard for me to breathe. I'm already overcome with nostalgia. I can feel it even if I don't yet know the word for it. It's hidden deep inside me, waiting in ambush in my heart to assault me. I'll think about it later perhaps, if I have time, if my life is ever comfortable enough for this strange feeling to express itself. . . . But here, right now, it's out of the question. . . . A sense of urgency is already compelling me to go back outside. The apartment's empty—no one's in there waiting for me.

When we got to the Vélodrome d'Hiver, Mama was upset with herself for having forgotten her change purse on a chair near the door. When the two guys told us to get ready, she began to gather the small amount of cash she had placed somewhere in her bedroom closet. She had left her change purse there, on a chair, no doubt thinking that she'd pick it back up and slip it into her coat pocket on her way out. . . . Her eyes staring at the cycling track, I can still remember her repeating: "What a fool I am! I forgot to take money!" She wouldn't have needed it, anyway. She'd only have ended up handing it over to the young militiamen who robbed us in the camp, or else she would have thrown it in a pail of excrement, like the three bills I pulled out. I reassure Mama: No one's been in our apartment since July 16; the purse is still on the chair. "There's no need to blame yourself. That money is yours, and it will be there when you get back."

I brush my hand over the *mezuzah* before I go back down the stairs. The object has no meaning for me. It's just a roll of parchment, and what's ever written on it in Hebrew I can't understand. Is our apartment really under God's protection because this piece of paper is nailed to the doorway? I doubt it. Except that on the station platform at Beaune-la-Rolande, among the shouts, the tears, in the midst of all the madness, I didn't say goodbye to Mama. Touching our door and caressing the *mezuzah* now are ways of talking to her, ways of saying, "You see? I'm home again. Everything is OK with me now."

Back in the street, I try to organize my thoughts to figure out where to go. Let's see, if Papa were to whisper in my ear, what advice would he give me? The Rue Cauchois, of course! Père Fabri's café! Just a few weeks ago, when we had become undesirables everywhere in our own city, he welcomed us, even with our yellow stars.

It's a beautiful summer's day, and the door is wide open onto the street. Standing behind his counter, Père Fabri opens his eyes wide when he sees me.

"Joseph! Come inside quickly, Joseph!"

It's early afternoon. No one's in the café. He closes the door behind me, grabs me by the shoulders, and takes my face in his hand as if to make sure it's really me.

"Joseph, are you all alone?"

"We were all arrested. Papa, Mama, my sisters, and me."

"Yes, I know. I mean, I know now. Too late, unfortunately. They rounded up more than 10,000 Jews in Paris."

"I saw them. We were all taken to the Vélodrome d'Hiver."

"And your parents, your sisters . . . where were they taken?"

"First to a camp, in Beaune-la-Rolande. Then they were put in a train and told they were going to the border, to Germany, or

to Poland. No one really knows. I couldn't go with them. After
that, I escaped."

Père Fabri is speechless. He locks the door and pushes me
toward the little room behind the kitchen. "You must be hungry. Come, I'll make you a bowl of soup. How does turnip
soup sound? I still have a few bowlfuls. Sit down and tell me
everything."

I found the right person. The entire time I'm telling my story,
Père Fabri shakes his head from left to right, sighing that it's
not possible. However, I avoid telling him the painful parts,
not to spare him but rather to make it less difficult for myself.
Then, I'm exhausted. For the first time since I escaped from
the camp of Beaune-la-Rolande with Joe, I finally feel I can let
down my guard. Alone with Père Fabri in his kitchen, I allow
myself a few tears.

"Listen, Joseph. We've got to get organized. To start with, I
still have a free bedroom upstairs, in the hotel. Go rest."

I sleep like a log. But when Père Fabri awakens me, at seven
o'clock in the evening, I don't like the serious look on his face.

"Joseph, I'm very sorry. You can't stay here."

In a fraction of a second, I understand. He doesn't want any
trouble, either. He's throwing me out like the others, and he'll
probably take me to the police precinct.

"Joseph, there's a guest register for the hotel. They inspect it
every day. But don't worry: I found a very nice lady who'll take
you in. I told her everything, and she's waiting for you."

I heave a huge sigh of relief. So he's not sending me back out
into the street. He's not going to turn me in. Hand in hand, like
father and son, Monsieur Fabri and I march up toward Sacré-
Coeur, to the Rue Saint-Rustique. We enter a little lopsided
house. The ground floor is divided into two apartments. We
knock on the door on the left. He leaves me there in the care of

a woman who seems disposed to do everything to help me. She has made a bed for me in an alcove, and I curl up in it right away. For a whole week, I stay there, without moving, without going outside even once. I don't feel the heat or my legs falling asleep. I feel no anger, no desire to confront her. Not moving suits me. I think I can wait here doing nothing until my parents return. I hardly ever see the woman who's taking care of me, even when she's there, present in the room. Is it because of my silence that she decides I have to leave?

One day she announces, "Joseph, now you have to go to the orphanage in the Rue Lamarck."

I accept what she says without saying a word.

"I'm not abandoning you. You'll be safer there. And I promise I'll come see you."

She must have thought that it would be better for me to be with children my own age. And it's true that I gradually awaken from my torpor there. For the first few days, I observe how this new camp functions. I obey the rules, participate in the shared chores, get up and go to bed when I'm supposed to, greet the Director, and say thank you when I get my piece of bread. When I've finally understood that we're all in the same situation, all unhappy at being separated from our families, I begin to confide in others. André Schwarz-Bart, a boy three years older than me, comes to ask me a few questions.

"I hear you were in Beaune-la Rolande."

"Yeah. You, too?"

"Yes. They let me out because I had tuberculosis. And you? Were you sick, too?"

"No. I escaped."

"That was you? There were two of you, right? You went underneath the barbed wire."

I say yes. He laughs and gets angry at the same time.

"Well, kid, maybe you consider yourself a hero. But you'll get no thanks from me. They never stopped bothering us because of you. You can't imagine the rage they were in. After that, they never stopped counting us, over and over again. There were so many of us that they kept losing their place, so they'd start all over again. And any time one of us went near the barbed wires, there was hell to pay, believe me. . . ."

"I believe you, I believe you! And I'm really sorry for you and the others. But you'll never make me regret getting out of there!"

Little by little, my story makes its way around the orphanage. I put the most painful images out of my mind—like being torn away from my parents at Beaune-la-Rolande on August 7—and hold on only to those of my escape two days later. I feel as though I won the war all by myself. The Germans had planned a fate for me that wasn't of my choosing. Having avoided it, having made all the guards in the camp fail, reassures me that I did more than play a dirty trick on them. I'm only an eleven-year-old kid, son of a Polish tailor. I have no weapons and I didn't kill anyone, but I was victorious over the brutes who persecute Jews.

We all realize that the adults who work all around us do everything possible to tend to our needs, but that's not enough to keep us calm. Lots of the boys have nightmares. Many nights are interrupted by screams that the children can't hold back: they're terrified as, in a troubled sleep, they relive their parents' arrest or something even worse. Once they're awake, they feel safe—but they're wrong. We're fed and the building is well heated, but we're all in danger. The Germans' short visits from time to time furnish ample proof: they never fail to leave without a few of us.

The Germans fill their notebooks with very precise numbers. They keep careful count of the Jewish children in Paris. They want to know where they are at every moment, so that they can do with them as they wish. No one has any illusions about their intentions anymore: they're bad. When a child is called into the Director's office or is summoned to pack up his things and follow the men in ogres' boots, he knows. One of them was sobbing loudly. It was embarrassing in front of the high authorities of the Occupation. A woman from the orphanage murmured to him, "Don't worry. You're going to go see your mother."

The poor little boy had almost stopped breathing, practically in a panic: "You're sure?"

"Yes, the soldiers told me."

"But Mama is dead!"

Did she die before the war? Or had this boy decided that she was dead because she hadn't been at his side for months? I'll never know, just as I won't know the fate of the others who left with him. I observe myself from a distance, almost distrustful of the person I'm becoming. But what choice do I have? The only thing I can think of is saving my skin. If I had stayed in the camp to hold the hand of a little one who had lost everything, where would I be now? Up to now, thinking about myself without feeling too much sympathy for the suffering of others has worked well for me. It's the law of the jungle, and I submit to it. Especially since the adults in the orphanage do their best to protect us.

———

"Joseph, we've decided to place you in a foster family."

"All right, Mr. Director, sir."

"They're very nice people, you'll see. They're quite well off."

I don't ask any questions. Besides, it wouldn't make any difference. I wait to see who I'm going to be dealing with.

I like the woman right away. She's beautiful, elegant, refined, and gentle in both her words and her actions. And she has a happy disposition to top it all off. Her husband, a lawyer, doesn't spend much time in their sumptuous apartment: an unending string of rooms, all decorated with delicate furniture, soft carpets, and heavy curtains on the windows. Every day, an old woman is there, the husband's mother, whom everyone calls "Grandmother," and Léontine, the maid, with her cap on her head and her pretty little apron always carefully ironed. . . .

A bedroom has been set up just for me. Suddenly I find myself sleeping in a big bed, like a prince. Books cover my nightstand, a fragile and precious lamp sheds a gentle light, and the closet is full: As soon as I moved in, Madame took me to her tailor. We went downstairs to a huge basement stocked with rolls of British fabric, both luxurious and sturdy. They made me a pair of knickers that must have cost a fortune—I prefer not to know. . . .

Weeks pass, and I regain confidence. The lady of the house asks me to call her *maman*, and I explain to her as gently as I can that I'm keeping that name for my real mother. So we come up with a compromise: I'll call her *mamine*. By her side, I feel myself becoming a normal child again. Until one day Léontine comes to get me in my room.

"Joseph, Grandmother would like to see you."

I walk to the living room, without any particular concern. Her daughter-in-law is there, visibly agitated, already worried about what is going to follow.

"Joseph," the old woman begins, standing, supported by her cane, . . . "Joseph, you took one of my rusks."

"What? No, madame, I didn't take any rusks."

"I know you did. I counted them, and one is missing. Why did you take it without asking me?"

"Madame, I assure you. . . ."

"Admit that you stole it, and it will be over and done with."

"But I can't, because I didn't take it!"

A terrible scene follows. While I'm crying because of this unjust accusation, Madame is crying about my future. Does she realize that her mother-in-law cooked up this whole story to get me thrown out of the house? Does she think that I really stole the rusk, and has she already forgiven me?

In any case, the next morning I'm back in the Rue Lamarck orphanage. Mamine, so sweet and gentle, won't be coming at night anymore to kiss me tenderly in my bed. We won't be walking hand in hand in the fancy neighborhoods. I won't be sitting next to her reading in front of the fireplace. The fairy tale is all over without my having been able to prove my innocence. I didn't see the old lady's plot coming, this old woman in a black dress, with her hair pulled back and her air of total serenity. Because of me, they neglected her, so she got rid of me.

So here I am, alone in the world again. I'm not upset at having to give up material comfort that I didn't even have time to get used to: it's Mamine's tenderness that I miss most. Little Joseph may be a hero, a real tough guy hunted by the Nazis everywhere on the planet, but he still needs love like everyone else.

—⁓—

Back to the orphanage, but not for long. Of all the children there, I'm certainly the most problematic. Maybe the most distressing as well: I'm filled with anxiety that I'll be found and sent back to a camp, and I communicate this feeling unconsciously to the other boys. I'm in perpetual motion: I want to be everywhere and hear everything at the same time. Of course, none of us can breathe easy, but I'm one of the most worried.

New destination: the Orgemont housing development, in Argenteuil, Seine-et-Oise. A couple asked to take in a boy. Good deeds can pay off: The UGIF, or Union Générale des Israélites de France, a Jewish charitable organization that oversees the orphanages, offers generous compensation to foster families. This time I'm placed with a railroad worker whose heart is as empty as his wallet. I arrive at his apartment with the Jules Verne books that Mamine gave me and depart a week later relieved of my treasure: Apparently I looked at a basketful of shriveled apples with the shifty eyes of a potential thief.... The Vichy government's propaganda has done its work: it seems as though I alone embody the danger posed by the Jews.

A few days later, two other boys and I are placed in a family residing on the Rue de la Pompe, in the sixteenth arrondissement. The bare minimum has been organized to house us: a bed to sleep in and an extra place at the table. We don't ask for more. But one afternoon, the couple's older son, who works for the UGIF, alerts his parents. "They're looking for all of you! Everyone has to get out of here as soon as possible!"

Everyone? My friends and I, transfixed, watch the spectacle of our host family packing up their bags as quickly as they can, wishing us good luck, and abandoning us there, among the furniture, like some kind of worthless objects.

"What are we going to do? Do we leave, too?"

As for me, I don't hesitate for a second. I fly down the stairs and head straight to the orphanage. My pals don't wait long to join me. Back to square one.

Soon afterward, a good woman from a distant suburb arrives to take three boys. I'm immediately chosen to be part of the group. My two comrades and I sit across from her in the director's office. She outlines the facts.

"Where I live isn't quite the countryside, but it's not far from it. I have a little house with a garden. There are chickens, rabbits, and, just behind the house, a big field where you can play as much as you want."

She describes her rural life to us so well that we organize a quick private chat behind her back. We're real city kids, with no desire to breathe in fresh air. One of my friends takes matters into his own hands.

"Listen, guys. We take the train with her. At the first stop, when they're just about to close the doors, we make a run for it!"

The other two do, in fact, take off, but not me. I have no more desire than they do to exile myself from civilization, but I don't feel that I'm in a position to be picky. It's five months now since my parents left, and I've had no news of them, just as there's no news of everyone else who took the same train, or the one the day before, or the day after. . . . 1942 is almost over, but not the war. I have no idea how much longer I'm going to have to hide. All I know is that each new day is one day closer to the end. If I stay with this woman, maybe I'll be able to accumulate a few more, and—who knows?—make it through to the end of this terrible time.

"Are you staying with me?"

"Uh . . . yes, Madame."

"Can you believe it? These people—we try to help them, and they don't let us!"

"These people?" That's what she calls us? These people? That's what I, too, am for this woman? I'm one of *these people*? I have an immediate negative reaction, and the little voice in my head, always faithful, warns me right away: *Joseph, this is another situation that's going to end badly. Get out of here!*

I take a train in the other direction and return to the orphanage. . . .

⎯⎯⎯

The director of the Rue Lamarck orphanage despairs. "Joseph, what are we going to do with you?"

This time, I don't answer. Not a single word. I'm so fed up with living like this. I didn't ask anyone for anything. I didn't ask for there to be a war, I didn't ask to be imprisoned in a camp, I didn't ask to be separated from my parents, I didn't steal a rusk, and most of all, I didn't ask to be Jewish!

"Listen, Joseph. I'm going to talk to someone at the Rothschild Foundation orphanage. It's bigger, and you'll be safer."

If he says so....

It's true that it's bigger: a city within the city, with its own school, kitchens, dormitories, and even a synagogue. I was born right here, in the hospital that I discover. Women still come to give birth here, with their stars on their chests. Don't they know that it's dangerous? That this little piece of fabric is all it takes for us to be picked up? Besides, I don't understand why I still have to wear mine. I can see that I'm not considered an ordinary resident, though. I spend my days reading and strolling through the hallways of the institution; I wander into the kitchens and take a nap leaning on the radiators. Apparently, a hero doesn't have to go to school. I don't miss it, I can tell you that!

The director leads the prayers in the synagogue on Saturdays, an opportunity for me to make the others jealous: He takes me under his prayer shawl, as if I'm more important than the other children. As if I'm the living proof of the existence of God. As far as I can tell, though, it's not God who tore up the skin on His hands, His head, and His back in the barbed wire of Beaune-la-Rolande.... One day just before the service, I tell the director of my fears.

"Monsieur, I'm not comfortable here."

"Really, Joseph? Why?"

"I don't know how to put it into words.... I think it's too easy for the Germans. We're ... we're all here in one place, day and night. They know where to find us to take us away!"

"But they don't because they don't have the right to. I can assure you that you don't have to be afraid. Here you're under the protection of the UGIF. There's nothing to worry about."

I'm not convinced, but what else can I say? I'm afraid of everything, everywhere, all the time—probably a normal reaction after all I've been through. Besides, I'm not the only one in my situation. The others might not be heroes, but their hearts are torn apart just like mine. Every day, they wait for a letter that never comes. You can often see them staring off into space.

A winter night in the beginning of 1943 brings proof that the danger is real for all of us, even under the protection of the UGIF and the Rothschild Foundation. The pounding of boots wakes us out of a sound sleep. Walking heavily, men suddenly enter the orphanage. There are a lot of them, and they post themselves at the entrance of several dormitories. Some children are ordered to get dressed as quickly as possible.

"Line up two by two. Downstairs!"

They're arrested. They cry, scream, and tremble like leaves. Terrified, they move close together. From my bed, still plunged into darkness, I hear everything. It's as though I can see what is happening to my friends. I know that they have the same panic-stricken looks on their faces and the same confused gestures that we had in the camp of Beaune-la-Rolande when our parents were taken away. The Germans open the doors. There's yelling and banging everywhere. I sit on my bed holding my breath, my pajamas buttoned up to my neck. Everything takes place in a few minutes. They have their quota of Jews for this visit. Silence once again falls on the orphanage, interrupted only by the sobs of a small child, terrorized by the arrest he just avoided, terrorized in advance at the thought of the next roundup.

The next day they tell me that there really weren't that many Germans and that, luckily, they were in a hurry. They also tell me that they went into every dormitory. Except mine.

Once again, I don't wait for the blessing of any adult to go else-where. Early in the morning, I find too many empty spaces on the benches in the Rothschild orphanage dining hall. I quickly make my way back to the Rue Lamarck. Seeing me there again, the director doesn't even try to hide his annoyance.

"Joseph! You again! What happened this time?"

"Last night . . . they came to take children from the Roths-child orphanage."

He remains silent a moment.

"I'm sorry, Joseph, . . . we're going to try to find some way to get you out of here. Somewhere really far away. Outside Paris, I promise."

On July 16, as soon as we arrived at the Vélodrome d'Hiver, Mama sent me to go look for her two brothers. I wandered around the entire place and didn't find them. Where are they today? I have no way of knowing, just as they certainly have no idea where their sister and her family are. I can't count on anyone, and there's no one who'll pay attention to my despair—first of all, because I'm not the only one who feels so unhappy, but also because grown-ups don't have the time or desire to lis-ten. I live in a world at war where Jews are treated like animals, where children disappear in the middle of the night, where adults and children don't encounter one another. I might as well get used to it. I evoke the imaginary cloak that I had cov-ered my family with at the Vél' d'Hiv. This time it falls on only my shoulders, and it brings no comfort. It just helps me to wait for tomorrow, then the next day, if my luck holds out.

7 · Three "Misérables"

Madame Clément is a little woman about fifty years old. She travels a lot for her work, looking for people all over France, but preferably at a good distance from Paris, who are willing to take Jewish children into their homes. She asks them about their motives, considers their resources, and evaluates their capacity for affection—in these three areas, she obviously is easily satisfied—and if she feels she can trust them, she brings them children.

This morning I'm in the train with Madame Clément. We're on our way to the Sarthe with two girls: Léa Cohen, ten years old, and Judith, barely twelve. The two sisters never leave each other's side. The younger one grasps onto her older sister as if she's a life preserver. She doesn't speak much: she's a little lost waif in a country at war. Judith makes it her responsibility to comfort Léa. She bears her burden with tenderness, realizing that it's a real stroke of luck not to be separated from her younger sister.

The girls don't know where their parents are, either, especially since they got divorced a few years earlier. The mother held onto her sons. Judith and Léa don't talk about their father, who took care of them on his own once the war started. They say he was arrested. The word has no meaning for them—it just frightens them terribly. They've never seen the cattle cars that take Jews to *Pitchi Poï*.

From experiencing roundups in the orphanages, from hearing other children tell their stories—the arrest of their parents, of their big brothers considered men even if they're not eighteen yet—I am absolutely sure of one thing: we have to hide the fact that we're Jewish from everyone, by every possible means. With our first names, that's not going to be easy. . . . I take advantage of a moment when we're alone together in the train to create new identities for us.

"Listen up, girls. Starting right now, we're no longer Joseph, Judith, and Léa. Those names are too Jewish. Léa, since your name starts with L, you'll be Liliane. Judith, let's say your name is . . . Jacqueline. And I'm René, OK?"

"How come you're not keeping your initial?" Judith asks me. "Why not Jean-Jacques?"

"Uh . . . that's just the way it is!"

They look at each other as if they think their fellow escapee is a real nitwit. It doesn't even occur to me that our last names are enough to raise suspicions. Jacqueline and Liliane Cohen sound very French to me! The same for René Weismann. I'm convinced that with these names, we won't be asked embarrassing questions by the other schoolchildren in the village where we're going to live. The best thing to do if you're going to avoid trouble is not to have to lie.

We follow Madame Clément through the main street of the village. The first stop is only for Léa: she's greeted by a family that wanted only one child, preferably a girl. Léa begins to whine, and we reassure her: Judith will be close by, in the house next door. They'll be together every day except at mealtimes and, of course, at night. And their separation is only temporary, we add.

"Judith! Joseph! You'll come to see me in a little while?"

I answer her with a frown: "Jacqueline and René, don't forget. We'll see you very soon, Liliane."

Now it's our turn to enter our new home. It's only one room, but big enough for a table and several beds. Behind it we can make out a tiny kitchen, that's all. We immediately sense that we're not welcome. With her ugly face, raspy voice, and rustic dialect, the lady of the house resembles a witch from another era in every detail. I feel as though I've gone back in time a hundred years. Does this woman at least have a heart inside her carcass? As soon as we've spent a couple of days with her, I can see that the answer is definitely no. In fifth grade, I studied a few passages from *Les Misérables*, by Victor Hugo. Well, Judith and I seem to have been sent to write the sequel to the story. It takes place in the Sarthe, in 1943, as the Germans bomb the south of France and treat Jews, from the oldest to the youngest, like animals.

Judith and I call this Madame X the old lady, or simply, the mother. She doesn't talk to us except to order us around and mistreat us. Whatever she asks us to do, we obviously don't get it right. She asked for a boy to do the work that her son, a prisoner of war, isn't there to do. I understand, and I perform my duties without balking. I go into the nearby woods to gather dead branches to burn in the fireplace, carry pails of water, and clean the outdoor toilets.

Judith has her share of chores, too, but she has a harder time putting up with them. A few days spent in the stench and excrement at the Vélodrome d'Hiver, followed by my experiences at the camp of Beaune-la-Rolande, prepared me well for this new ordeal. Judith hasn't gone through anything like this. Before ending up in the Rue Lamarck orphanage, she lived with her father. The anti-Jewish laws prevented him from working toward the end, and he could provide her only the most rudimentary material comfort, but the only world she knows is one where adults carried out their responsibilities with dignity and without malice toward children.

The atmosphere at the table at mealtime is exactly like that described by Victor Hugo in his book. The room is dark and the soup is thin—I can't even describe the flavor. Everyone is bent over his plate, and no one speaks. In my house, too, we lived frugally, and perhaps without the best manners, but neither my sisters nor I would ever have allowed ourselves to make so much noise with our mouths while eating. In this house, it appears that all the inhabitants can do whatever they want—and there are a lot of them. Besides the old lady, there's her very beautiful daughter Raymonde and several grandchildren who come and go without ever staying for long. They never talk to us. Do we scare them? They know nothing about us except that we're from Paris and we're going to stay there for a while, but no one knows how long. Did the mother tell them we're Jewish? We don't want to have any more to do with them than they with us: we have no desire to talk or to explain anything. They're brutes like their grandmother. They probably feel contemptible anyway, because they never raise their eyes to look at us, just steal an occasional glance.

Léa-Liliane, having found out from her sister how the shrew mistreats us, asked to join us. She feels guilty living in comfort and kindness while her sister cries herself to sleep every night. Too bad the move didn't go in the other direction. . . . At least the girls and I form a good team now. I'm a few months older than Judith, and I can manage much better than both sisters, whatever the circumstances. I'm becoming a kind of older brother to them, and I protect them as much as I can. We stick together.

In the fall of 1943, we're enrolled in the local school. The schoolmaster is obviously delighted to have such a joyful

Parisian kid in his class. I decide to make all the children in the village our allies. They're just as rough and unsophisticated as the old lady's grandchildren, but at least they aren't cruel to us. Their parents are butchers, farmers, and policemen, and the kids have known each other since they were born. They don't know I'm Jewish—not one of them has asked. Do they even know what a Jew is? They go to mass every Sunday, and for them Jews are bad people who crucified their sweet Jesus. Another era. . . . Nothing to do with me, the new kid, the life of the party, always ready to make my pals laugh. We play tag, cops and robbers, and Duck, Duck, Goose together. We run around in the street, go fishing, and steal apples in the orchards.

On Sundays, we meet up on the same benches in the church. Only Léa sits in the front, as close as possible to the altar. She has fallen hopelessly in love with God. Everything she endures is for Him. I've been made to understand clearly that I don't deserve anything good on this earth because I was born Jewish. Léa prefers to think that she's suffering in order to be worthy of a place next to God the Father. Why not? Unfortunately, the old lady, holier-than-thou on Sundays, a depraved sinner the rest of the week, encourages our dear Lili in her self-abnegation by punishing her severely for the slightest thing.

When Madame Clément comes to see us, about once every three months, she brings us chocolates, sugar cubes, and candy. . . . She gives them to the shrew, who is supposed to hand them out to us sparingly. Of course, her daughter and her grandchildren get to eat much more of them than we do. Judith and I have no scruples about taking what's supposed to be for us. We climb up on a stool, open the old box where the goodies are tucked away, and serve ourselves discreetly. With Léa, we're as harsh as older brothers and sisters can be. As she watches us lick our fingers, we tell her to climb up herself.

"We're not giving you any! You know where the candies are. Go get them yourself!"

"Stealing is a sin. The priest said so!" she announces furiously.

"Madame Clément brought the candy for us. For the three of us. The old lady's the thief, not us!"

Convinced by our argument, Léa slips into the little room behind the kitchen. She climbs up as best she can on a stepladder, stands on her toes to reach the infamous box, and sneaks a few sugar cubes before putting everything back in place. She keeps them in her blouse all day, savoring the moment when she can slide them into her mouth, once night has fallen. It really wasn't that hard. . . .

Alas, the old lady smells a rat and goes to check on the munitions. The woman never went to school, doesn't know how to read or write, but she knows how to count her pennies and any other form of wealth. Just before dinner, she inspects the troops—us, the three refugees. It's obvious that the members of her own family are above suspicion. Judith allows herself to be searched without saying a word. I turn my pockets inside out with no worries. As for Léa, she just says no without the slightest gesture. The mother seems fairly satisfied, and then Léa unfortunately denounces herself: "Have a look! I didn't take anything!"

She pulls out the handkerchief she had slipped in over the sugar in her pocket. The cubes, which had gotten stuck to the fabric, fall on the floor. Léa is petrified. The worst part is that the old lady doesn't even shout. She stares at the stolen objects on the floor, then raises her eyes toward Léa and lets out an evil laugh. Her shoulders move up and down, and she bares her half-rotten teeth in a contempt-filled sneer.

"So, Léa, since you love Our Lord so much, here's your punishment: You're gonna draw ten crosses on the floor—with your tongue, of course!"

Léa doesn't understand. Judith and I can only stand there and watch, speechless at the woman's despicable cruelty.

"Well, what're you waitin' for?"

"But . . . but . . . ," mumbles Léa, bursting into tears.

"Ten crosses I said!"

Of the three of us, Léa is Victor Hugo's Cosette. She gets on her knees, lowers her pretty face to the terra cotta squares, gray from ashes and dust, and begins her penitence. The other children snicker discreetly: they don't dare laugh too hard for fear that the old lady might turn on them as well. Judith cries in silence in a corner. As for me, I tighten my fists in a rage.

I never believed in God. I never had the time. When Mama fervently recited the prayers in the synagogue, I sat quietly by her side to please her, not to please God. Evidently, Léa gets the strength to endure life in this house from the Church. The fact that this vile woman sings so piously on Sunday and then treats a ten-year-old girl like this the rest of the week revolts me. God, if He exists, certainly doesn't appreciate it, either. . . . But I don't believe that God exists, and I know that this doesn't make me a bad person. In almost thirteen years of life, I've met so many men and women whose actions are contemptible. In my mind, I can see the militiamen at the camp of Beaune-la-Rolande, the Germans tearing children two years old out of their parents' arms, Mamine's mother-in-law and her allegedly stolen rusk, and now this heartless woman humiliating this child, who looks like a china doll, fragile and beautiful.

The signs of the cross traced on the floor by Léa's tongue will take hours to wear off. In vain, she stands back up with dignity and goes out without a word to wash out her mouth; in vain, she'll tell us that she did as God wanted: I already know that the memory of this moment will always remain in her mind and in her heart. Mistreatment of children creates wounds that never heal. It's the beginning of 1944, more than a year now that we've endured the nastiness and cruelty of this crazy old shrew. The war isn't over. Neither are the bullying and fear.

—⁓—

We call her the old lady, but she's probably not all that old. I think that she's gone rancid on the inside and that it's showing on the outside. I could have loved her, anyway. I arrived at her house with an empty heart. All it wanted was to be filled with love, which I would have returned a hundred times over. I would never have asked her to wear beautiful dresses like Mamine, or to put cream on her lips, so they'd be smooth and gentle, or to polish her nails. I understand that the way she lives and works isn't compatible with concern about her appearance, not to mention that she doesn't have the money, anyway. All she'd have to do is be fair and kind to us. Not even generous. Just . . . respectful.

I'm almost ashamed to use such a word. My parents taught me well: adults have a duty to take care of children, to protect them and therefore to respect them. And it's the children's duty to respect their elders. You respect your teachers, you respect the man who owns the hardware store, you respect the rabbi, the policeman, the beggar, the *schnorrer*. The Kraut? No, not him—he's the exception. If Papa and Mama could see how the old lady treats Judith, Léa, and me, would they allow me the right to hate her as I do? Would they think I'm pretentious because I think the she should treat the three of us in her care with a minimum of respect?

It's a Sunday in February, almost a holiday in the shrew's house. Her son and daughter who live in Paris have come to visit her. There's also a daughter who lives in the next village, with her own children, and Raymonde, the youngest. We're all seated around the table. Judith, Léa, and I are trying to make ourselves as invisible as possible. We don't talk much, and above all, we don't take part in the conversation unless we're invited, which rarely happens. Usually, when the old lady speaks to us, it's to send us to get wood or water, to bring over a chair, or to close the shutters. But on this occasion, she's decided to show some interest in us for some reason. Particularly merry, she asks us questions, certain that we're going to put on a good show with our very exotic replies.

"What do youse Jews do on Sunday?"

The girls don't answer. I'm the oldest, the man, so it's up to me to take risks. I accept my role willingly: if necessary, I'll have the required repartee. For the moment, it's best to keep a low profile.

"We don't do anything in particular."

"Ain't Sunday a holy day for you? Don't youse need to rest? So Jews never work?"

"My father works on Sunday. It's on Saturday that he doesn't work."

"Saturday! Fancy that!"

They all burst into laughter, as if I just said something hysterically funny. The mother continues to needle me with her questions.

"And what else does a Jew do?"

I want to answer her that a Jew washes his hands before sitting down to eat, that he says hello to his neighbors, that he reads books and kisses his children, unlike crazy old women like her that you meet in this God-forsaken part of the Sarthe. I want to spit in her face, to tell her that we're not like her in any way and that she only inspires contempt in me. Instead, I hold my tongue. In the look on Judith's face, I see the same advice that I'm giving myself in secret: Let it pass. With a bit of luck, she'll get tired of this subject and move on to something else. . . .

"We don't do anything. Nothing at all."

As innocent as it appears, this response is still not enough to stop her.

"Nothing? Youse is regular people just like us?"

"..."

"I know that youse ain't like us. Come on, show us what makes you a Jew!"

Is it because her children are there? Does she feel encouraged by their presence? Has the wine put her in a particularly good mood today? She gets up and approaches me. Then she grabs me by the shoulder.

"Come on! Show us!"

I pull away from her violently. I understand exactly what she wants. I know full well what part of my anatomy she thinks my Judaism resides in, and it's exactly that part of my body that my modesty forbids me to expose.

"No! No!"

I move away from the table, but she follows me. Even if she isn't big, she has the upper hand, because of the physical power that emanates from her robust body.

"For sure, you're gonna show us!"

"Leave me alone!"

"You ain't gonna make a big scene, are ya? Show us your thing!"

She tries to grab my pants near my belt. I fight back like crazy.

"Leave me alone I said!"

The old lady isn't playing around anymore. What began as an ugly farce has turned into a show of force. She intends to take power over me by brutality, since she has no influence on my independent character. As she pushes me down on the bed, I kick and punch her. She calls her children to the rescue.

"Get over here! Help me to hold him down!"

They laugh and encourage one another. One grabs me by the hair, another by the arms, which he folds behind my back. The old lady immobilizes my legs. I scream as loud as I can. What am I hoping for? That a neighbor will come to see what's going on here? My rage and my screams serve no purpose. How long has our struggle been going on? It seems like an eternity to me. I hurt everywhere, I'm terrorized, I'm crying, biting—nothing stops them. How can these brutes be so insensitive to my distress? My body belongs to me and to me alone. It's perhaps the last thing that remains from my life before: my child's body, just the way my parents created it. What did Papa ever do to me? Three or four taps on the head, and I had certainly deserved them. This old lady has already beaten me on the legs with a thin wooden stick. She flailed them relentlessly one evening after school, and the marks remained for weeks. It hurt, but it didn't affect me. While the blows fell on my calves, I thought to myself that the violence couldn't harm me, that I'd forget it, and that one day I'd forget this shrew as well.

But this time, it's different. I never felt so humiliated. They're attacking me fiercely, full of hostility and hate. What they're revealing to me in treating me this way is worse than contempt. The mother has unbuttoned my pants. Her joy erupts as she sees her victory so close at hand. Judith and Léa beg her to stop. There's indescribable chaos in the house. The entire space is filled with our shouts and crying. I can feel that my buttocks are uncovered, my private parts revealed. Raymonde, beautiful Raymonde, almost seventeen, a woman now, watches me with a mixture of amusement and greedy desire in her eyes. She inspires only disgust in me. I feel nauseated to be exposed to her and these monsters, her family, in this way.

The old lady wipes the sweat off her brow with the back of her hand. "That's it? It weren't nothin' to make such a big deal about!"

I put my clothes back on, sobbing. All my strength and even my anger have abandoned me. I feel like a marionette with broken joints. Judith and Léa have turned toward the wall and are crying silently. I'm glad that there's nothing that distinguishes them physically as Jewish girls. Like them, I cry tears that don't comfort me. The little voice in my head changes its tone. It calls me all kinds of names: *Stupid ass! Why did you escape? Look how unhappy you are now....*

Where's *Pitchi Poï*? I don't know how to get there. It's too late now to find my sisters and my parents.

8 · The Americans

Standing at his desk this morning, our teacher looks more solemn than usual. When he asked us to line up two by two in the courtyard a little while ago, we didn't notice anything in particular, except perhaps a slight smile below his mustache. But now that we're standing behind our chairs, we're curious. He's stiff as a board, hands behind his back, almost at attention. And strangely enough, he doesn't ask us to sit down. We're sure that he has some kind of news to tell us, something serious and extraordinary.

"Children, you probably already suspect that this is a special day, and it will remain so in the history of our country. . . . I heard yesterday on the wireless that the Americans have landed on the coast of Normandy!"

That's his earth-shattering news? None of us moves a muscle. We don't understand the significance of the teacher's words at all, and he doesn't wait to explain them. "The Americans have come to liberate France."

This time there's an explosion in the classroom. We let go of our chair backs and turn to one another, filled with both joy and disbelief. One boy shouts, "So we won the war?"

The teacher laughs, and so do the rest of us for a few seconds, even when he calls us back to order . . . and self-control.

"Calm down, children. Unfortunately, no. We can't say that we've won yet. While we wait for the Americans to make their way through the country and meet up with the Red Army moving in from the Eastern Front, we may even be in more danger. There may be bombing, for example. In a moment, I'll tell you how to stay safe if that happens."

No one cares about the bombing. We all share the same joy. But I swear that none of my classmates is more relieved than I am. I lift my head and throw out my chest—I feel as though I've just grown four inches. Suddenly I can see the end of my torment after being plunged into a nightmare for almost two years now.

On Wednesday, July 15, 1942, I fell asleep in the safety of my family's apartment for the last time. Since then, I've never felt completely at ease. I saw my father hold his head high as he faced the gendarmes, but I also saw him scream in rage and pain when the German soldiers tore me away from him. I saw my mother close her eyes at the sight of the half-naked woman the militiamen were kicking with their heavy boots. I saw the gates of the camp close behind my entire family. They all disappeared in a few seconds, and I couldn't even make them out through the curtain of my tears. Since then, I've had no news. Hidden in this little village in the Sarthe, in the home of this despicable woman, I've sometimes had doubts. I've thought that maybe I shouldn't have escaped from Beaune-la-Rolande but should have gone with my parents, to *Pitchi Poï* or wherever they are. But that feeling lasted only as long as the blow of a stick on my legs. Today, more than ever, as the teacher announces our approaching liberation, I know that I was right after all . . . in spite of the old woman's stupidity and cruelty.

All over the school, children are rejoicing, but none of them as much as Léa, Judith, and I. We have more to gain from this victory than all our classmates put together. I want so much to believe, that I don't doubt for an instant that my parents are going to come back, and I know that the girls also see no other possible outcome: soon we'll be back with our families.

One day, the ground trembles from all the vehicles crisscrossing the countryside. The Germans have begun to pack their bags. They're retreating. I'm outside the house with Judith, Léa, and a few of the old lady's grandchildren. The noise seems to be coming toward us. We hear more than motors—there are also crackling sounds, muted but more worrisome. The mother rushes out and tells us to go back inside. In a few seconds, the entire street is deserted. It's time. We can hear explosions far off; soon they're coming closer and closer. Shots are fired in one direction, then in the other: the Americans and the Germans are face to face, not too far off.

We all get down on the floor—the old lady, too. We stay this way for two hours, mostly in silence, as if we risk being discovered by some enemy if we talk too loud. I'm not afraid that bullets might pass through the heavy wooden door: I don't believe in accidents; instead I trust in luck. I know that right at this moment, the fact that I'm Jewish no longer means anything. I'm called René, and everyone, including my teacher, thinks that I'm from a family of real, pure-blooded Frenchmen. Except for Judith and Léa, to whom I've told my story, no one knows what I lived through at the Vél' d'Hiv or the camp at Beaune-la-Rolande. The old lady has seen what makes a Jew: only humiliation remains, no threats. In the house it's hot as hell, just like two years ago in the Vélodrome d'Hiver. But the floor is cool beneath me, and this time I can hear fighting outside—fighting for Judith, for Léa, and for me. Just for the three of us.

It's been quiet for a while now. We stand up gingerly, rubbing our hands to get the dust off. I approach the window and peek through a crack in the shutter. A small shape traverses the sky, but no one is concerned because it's a reconnaissance plane. . . . It disappears right away. Soon the village returns to life. We open the door and decide to risk going out onto the sidewalk. Our neighbors do the same. Everyone looks at each other, incredulous and impatient.

"What now?"

All we can hear is the sound of motors coming closer. The shooting seems to have stopped for good. We're waiting without knowing if there's anything to wait for. Groups form in the street. They discuss the situation, coming up with hypotheses—but never too far from their houses, in case they have to run back inside. I grab a piece of wood and begin to sharpen it. It's long enough to reach the apples on the highest branches. If I sharpen the point enough, it'll easily pierce the fruit: all I'll have to do is pull. . . .

I'm not worried about the outcome of the battle between the Americans and the Germans a few hours ago: I know the former won. No, I'm not panicking. They took several weeks to get here from the coast of Normandy. That means it's going to take days and days before the entire country is liberated and maybe even weeks before my parents return. I still have time to be hungry, and the apples have time to ripen.

I'm not able to finish sharpening my stick. It's been only two hours since the fighting ended, and vehicles are already approaching the village. Everyone rushes back inside in a flash, me last. But since there's no sound of gunshots over the humming of the engines, people peek out their doors . . . me first. I see a military car, a jeep, coming down the main street a few hundred meters from the house. A big, heavy gun is pointing forward, and a man is leaning on it—not really standing, but not bent over, either. The driver is next to him, and in the back, two men are holding onto bars on the sides. They're advancing very slowly, in silence. Another jeep follows them. I can make out another and then one more. Soon it's an unending procession.

Voices burst forth from the houses: "The Americans! It's the Americans!"

All fear having vanished into thin air, everyone goes out to watch our liberators pass by. While the entire village explodes in joy, Judith, Léa, and I fall into one another's arms and begin a St. Vitus dance like none anyone's ever seen before. Raymonde runs out to greet the jeeps, and everyone claps, shouts, and laughs like crazy. Even the old lady comes out to applaud the Americans! Standing resolutely on her two feet with her hands on her broad hips, she shakes her head from left to right as if she can't believe it. But I want to believe it! I leap like a goat. Judith, holding a big box of candy in her hands, cries tears of joy. She hands out her booty generously. I almost choke on a caramel! The soldiers throw packs of cigarettes, chewing gum, and little chocolate bars to whoever wants one. We all want one!

We wish this parade would never end. The entire village is in a state of euphoria at being invaded by these big, strong men, who are as happy as we are to be able to bring us such joy. Our wish has come true! For hours, hundreds and hundreds of jeeps, cars, and trucks cross through the village on their way into the countryside, before liberating another village, then another and another, then a city, lots of cities, and—I can already tell—Paris!

It's hard to go to bed tonight. At dinner the soup is as thin as ever. Stuffed by all the sweets that we're not accustomed to anymore—were we ever?—we hardly raise our spoons to our lips. To tell the truth, for the first time in a long while, we don't mind having empty stomachs, even after mealtime. The news has spread throughout the village: an American unit has set itself up in the castle, the same one the Germans had requisitioned three years earlier. I can't wait to go see. . . .

———

Our apartment at 54 Rue des Abbesses looked out on the back of a movie theater, Studio 28. We never had enough money to go there together as a family. But I remember that Mama once went to see a Charlie Chaplin film, *Modern Times*. Mama rarely went out of the house, only to go to the synagogue or do some shopping. . . . I imagine that Papa wanted just this once to offer her the pleasure of seeing a movie. She came home enchanted, her eyes still filled with tears.

"I laughed and laughed! You should have seen him with his mustache and his little hat. He's so clumsy—he does everything the wrong way and gets himself into all kinds of trouble."

Rachel interrupts Mama: "But that doesn't sound funny."

"Yes, it's funny because he doesn't care what happens to him. He's always dreaming. His head is constantly in the clouds, and he laughs at himself. You see, that way nothing seems serious to him."

Dear Mama, now that the Americans are here and the Germans are gone, I've decided to be like Charlie Chaplin. I'm going to become as happy as I used to be. I have two legs that can run fast and a head full of mischief. I can be of use to our new neighbors. After all, I was a guide for a Kraut not so long ago. . . . And I'm not afraid of the Americans. . . .

The American soldier's name is Jeff. Jeff Messer. His name
means knife in German. He thinks it's funny and jokes about
it every time I see him: "Joe! Moi American Kraut! *Achtung!*"

I've never told anyone I'm Jewish. You never know. . . .

Raymonde has gotten it into her head that Jeff is going to
marry her. Only one thing bothers her: He's a man, a real one,
who knows about women and what to do with them. So Raymonde is afraid to have sex with him. She would rather that I
deflower her: I'm thirteen with soft skin and a body that's still
slender and delicate. I won't hurt her too much. But I'm not
aware of all this at first . . . so I'm all the more surprised by her
behavior.

She starts out by following me everywhere: to the woods,
where I go to gather firewood, or to the fields, where I pull up
a few roots for the soup. She bumps into me, pushes me down
on the grass, rubs against me. I have no idea what she wants
from me, but I'm already terrorized. I get out of her clutches
as best I can, run off, and avoid her for the rest of the day. She
sneaks up behind my back when I go to pee in the outhouse.
She wants to see and she tries to arouse me—at least that's what
she thinks she's doing. Since I've never thought about all this,
I have no reaction.

"Don't you think I'm pretty enough for you?"

"Of course. You're beautiful, Raymonde. But what do you
want from me?"

"I want you to do it with me, one time."

"You want me to do what?"

"Take my virginity, of course!"

So that's what's been going on. . . . What a crazy idea! I try to
persuade her that I'm not old enough for such things yet, but
none of my arguments seems to convince her. I'm just a kid, I

have no idea how to go about it, and most of all, I haven't got the slightest desire to do so. Raymonde will hear none of it. She's decided that I have to obey her in this matter the same way I obey the old lady for household chores. After all, for her I'm part of the inferior race: By what right could I refuse to take her virginity? She thinks she's doing me a favor!

The weeks pass, and her demands become more and more pressing. Not a day goes by that she doesn't trap me against a wall. She slips her hands between my legs and brushes her pelvis against mine. I defend myself with difficulty, unable to solicit help from anyone else, especially not the mother. Her daughter would say that I tried to rape her, and I'd be beaten more severely than ever.

One night, unable to wait any longer, Raymonde takes advantage of our forced promiscuity to launch a serious attack. In the house's single room, we sleep spread across three beds every night: the biggest is for the old lady and her two youngest grandchildren, a narrower one is for Judith and Léa, and I sleep in the last, between Jeannot, the oldest of her grandsons, and Raymonde. Once everyone's asleep, she throws herself on me, traps me on my back, and straddles me. I twist around to turn onto my side and pull my knees up to my chest, at least as much as the narrow bed allows. Jeannot, disturbed in his sleep, elbows me furiously. Raymonde attempts a new offensive. She slides her hand into my underwear and caresses me clumsily, especially since I'm doing contortions to try to escape from her. I'm frozen in fear that she might achieve her goal. I'm convinced that her vagina is hiding razor-sharp teeth ready to bite the first dick that passes by. Whatever maneuvers this maniacal girl attempts, my penis gets so small that I imagine it will disappear completely before daybreak. All night long, without ever tiring, she throws herself into the fray. Each time I fight her off, careful not to make any noise that would wake someone up: shame combines with my fear. The old lady turns over in her sleep. Once she even says to her daughter, "What the heck are you moaning about?"

In the morning, I jump out of bed, exhausted but relieved at having succeeded in preserving my family jewels in spite of Raymonde's doggedness. From that moment on, she can't stand me. She doesn't try to trap me in a corner anymore—she's given up. Instead she increases her daily harassment, trying to get me into trouble if something is broken, if the table isn't set on time, if the pitcher is empty—she's deliberately poured out its contents. One day, on the pretext that I had picked more pears from a tree than I brought home, she grabs a switch, a thin piece of wicker as sharp as a knife blade, and decides to punish me. I scream and cry. The blows to my downy child's legs don't let up, and blood runs down my calves to my ankles. The pain is so bad that soon I no longer feel anything. Raymonde has avenged herself.

Jeff goes off with his unit; he's left her behind, in her misery. I grit my teeth. It's official now: We've won the war. It won't be long before my parents come for me. I'll return to buy the newspaper at the corner of Rue des Abbesses and Rue Tholozé. I'll read the news myself, while Raymonde remains in this hole. As beautiful as she is today, she'll grow old like her mother. She doesn't yet have her flabby, repulsive body, but the same spite already rushes through her veins. What do the blows to my legs matter? By the time the wounds heal, I'll be far from here.

9 · The Castle of Méhoncourt

I never have to see the old lady or her crazy daughter again. A car parks in front of the house to pick up Judith, Léa, and me. A man gets out and asks the mother to gather our belongings. We haven't been told, so this is a wonderful surprise. What difference does it make where they take us? My two half-sisters and I have all experienced our share of humiliation in this village. But today a new era in our lives is beginning, and we know instinctively that it's going to be happier than the one that's ending. Everything will take on a new character. We're leaving behind a life of oppressed prisoners. We don't think about it too much, but we feel a sense of profound relief at not being dirty Jews anymore. We're going to be what we were before the war again: regular children, like all the others.

We get in the car. The man stares at us one after the other, but we don't ask any questions. Are we going to his house? Is he going to place us in a new family? Are we going home? Does he know where our parents are, now that the Germans have left the country? Our silence in the presence of our savior is odd. All these questions are stirring in our minds, but they don't make it to our lips—as though we somehow sense that this man's responses wouldn't be what we want to hear.

We quickly travel the twelve or so miles to the Castle of Méhoncourt, outside the town of Le Mans. Dozens of other children have been gathered there, and dozens more will soon arrive. We mix in with them with indescribable happiness. Soon we'll make friends, we'll tell each other our stories, we'll embellish our memories from before the war and make the dark hours sound worse than they were. But we already know why we're together here: first of all, we're Jewish; second, we've been separated from our parents; finally, we're living on hope. We're all in total ignorance of what has happened to our families. All I know is that I saw mine go off in the direction of the Beaune-la-Rolande railroad station. Others remember only the day their parents were arrested. They didn't go with them—it was at the start of the German occupation, when they weren't yet arresting children. They were handed over to the UGIF, then hidden in the homes of different people, until they, too, were brought to the castle, the last transit point before returning to their families. In spite of the profound anxiety deep inside each of us, we're happy, quite simply, because we're alive. No one's explained anything to us, and we're not asking any questions. But we all know instinctively, in our guts, in this autumn of 1944, that the very fact that we can smell the odor of wet grass constitutes a major victory.

A dormitory has hastily been built in a room in the castle. For now, we have only mattresses on the floor. The walls still bear the stigmata of the German presence. They marked them up with swastikas, probably just before they left. That doesn't make them the victors. . . . The castle belongs to a Jew who has disappeared, sent to a camp in all likelihood, and it has been turned over for now to the Oeuvre de Secours aux Enfants, the OSE, which helps Jewish orphans.

"Orphan" is a word I refuse to use to describe myself. Of course, I'm living in an orphanage, yet I don't consider myself to be alone in the world. The last time I saw my parents they were as alive as I am. . . .

I think my buddies and I are all doing the same thing: we're waiting for their return without asking ourselves too many questions. After having spent years trying to imagine what our parents are eating, what kind of beds they're sleeping on, how they spend their days—after failing to be able to form pictures of them in our minds, in *Pitchi Poï* or anywhere else, we've all stopped looking for answers. We're waiting for them, and we'll ask them what we've always wanted to know when they return.

For now, I'm satisfied to be learning something. They want me to be a machine tool fitter? I'll be a machine tool fitter. A few months later, I learn carpentry. Why not? I like wood. Hmm . . . we haven't yet tried sheet metal worker. Okay, let's twist and work some zinc to make gutters. . . . While the others walk calmly to middle or high school, a whole group of us sets off every morning for vocational school. In the evening, we return to the orphanage like workers returning to their homes, backs broken, hands dirty, minds numb from the exhausting work we've just completed. The director keeps a close eye on me. He tells me as much. I feel threatened again. But why? And by whom exactly?

Every day the Americans walk past the gate of the castle and throw us chewing gum, which we grab while it's still in the air. The director collects as much as he can to distribute to us sparingly. Even though I try to cooperate in every way, it seems to me as though I never get as much as the others. The worst part is that I feel hurt even though I don't really even like the taste of chewing gum. I'm greedy for something else: for love, a bit of tenderness, perhaps the slightest hint of affection. Nothing comes my way. Feelings don't fall out of a truck in little cubes wrapped in silver paper. They aren't scattered by the wind like tiny crumbs of bread thrown to the birds. They can't be found in the tools that my child's hands work so hard to lift in the workshop or the factory. A pat on the head, on my shoulder, a smile or a wink would be enough for me. Monsieur T. has better things to do, more pressing issues to deal with than my need for love. The months pass, and there are still just as many orphans at Méhoncourt.

———

Since the Liberation, the OSE has increased its efforts to reunite families, in collaboration with the Ministère des Prisonniers de Guerre, Déportés et Rapatriés. But with the war, the arrests, the deportations, the need for the luckiest Jews to go into hiding, and the country's slow attempt to pull itself back together, it's difficult to find our close relatives. They're working on it—that's all we know, and all anyone wants to tell us. Nothing, however, about the few dozen men who returned from Auschwitz in April and May of 1944. Nothing, obviously about their extreme physical and psychological weakness. Nothing about the 12,884 people arrested on July 16 and 17, 1942, and locked up in the Vélodrome d'Hiver. The adults tell us nothing about the horrors they're beginning to hear about; they assure us only that they're working nonstop to find our loved ones. But the genealogists' work is complicated: certain last names, too common, often lead to dead ends.

Finally, my friends Léa and Judith find an aunt. She works for a Paris circus and is going to take them in. From time to time, a bell sounds in the lobby. Everyone stops talking and holds his breath until a name is pronounced. "Jacques, to the parlor!" He runs off, while the others—all the others—sigh in disappointment. Jacques will pack his bag in a flash and go off to live with a cousin, an uncle, or a family friend who comes to get him. Sometimes—rarely—a father comes to retrieve his son or daughter—a man who could be my own father, except that this particular man didn't trust the Vichy government. A man who had the presence of mind to hide his children at the very beginning of the German occupation and who went underground somewhere, waiting for better days.

And so the weeks and months go by. A hand rings the bell in the lobby of the castle, and it's never my name that's called to go to the parlor. I learn that not all adult Jews were taken away in trains. I'm happy for each of my friends who is reunited with his family, and yet I feel a kind of bitterness. I, Joseph Weismann, the escapee, the hero, am ashamed at the thought that my parents allowed themselves to be taken away so naïvely—and I feel ashamed of the shame I feel toward them. Nevertheless I still believe; I'm waiting for them. They never come, but, once again, luck reaches out its hand to me.

My good fortune presents itself in the person of a woman who owns a furniture store in Le Mans. Like so many others before and after her, she took a taxi to Méhoncourt, walked into the director's office, and spoke to him with simplicity and generosity.

"Monsieur, I know that the children here lack distractions. I'm offering to take a girl to my home, one day a week. She'll be able to play, eat well, and rest. We'll be like a second family to her."

Since I'm walking by, Mr. T. takes advantage of the situation: "Imp, come here a second, please."

"Bonjour, madame."

"Imp, go get Madeleine. She must be out in the garden right now."

Was it my natural politeness that won over the woman? In any case, when I return the office, with Mado on my heels, I'm the one she wants to take for an ice cream sundae. I choose the biggest one, a colossal *pêche Melba*. All the flavors mix together, and the whipped cream drips onto the table! This sundae is the most beautiful thing I've ever seen in my life. My benefactor laughs at my gluttony and seems to be holding back tears of emotion. I could tell her that it's no use worrying about me, that everything will be back to normal soon with the return of my parents, but what good would it do me? Especially since Madame Margel continues to come take me out from time to time. She's very kind, and the affection she shows me, even if it's discreet, warms my heart and soul.

The tradition among children in an orphanage is that you're allowed to enjoy what can't wait to be consumed, but wrapped candies have to be brought back for everyone to share. That's the rule at Lamarck, at the Rothschild Foundation, and at the Castle of Méhoncourt: all the beneficiaries of adult generosity obey it willingly. Madame Margel doesn't hold back when it comes to filling my pockets with candy. Every time I return from a day with her, my popularity rises with the booty I distribute.

Madame Margel seems ready to offer me everything she has: her home, where I'm welcomed as warmly by her husband as by her daughter; their furniture store, where I'll have a position if I wish—in short, a future. I'm not ready for anything. I'm not giving up my former life. Besides, no one's encouraging me to do so at the Castle of Méhoncourt. Once, and only once, I hear something that almost makes me admit the possibility that my parents might not be coming back. Dozens of children, including me, are in the garden. An American army truck stops outside the gate, just long enough to give out some candy, I guess. But something at the back of the truck attracts our attention. Several German soldiers are seated, guarded by American soldiers. Some kids start to throw stones at them. The children's cries come to the attention of Monsieur T., who joins us. The Americans scold us for throwing pebbles at the prisoners. Monsieur T. can't accept this. I discover that he speaks German and that his rage can fall on someone besides us, when we break a dish or a floor tile. He begins to scream at the prisoners. He shouts a few sentences in their language and a few more in ours.

I hear him accuse them: "You killed their parents!" And he includes us all in a sweeping gesture.

Killed? Surely not all of them! Our director is completely crazy. I'm not going to swallow such a huge lie. He must be talking about the war in general, about the French victims, about the parents of all the children of my generation. He can't mean Schmoul and Sara Weismann. It's impossible.

The truck drives off, the director returns to his office grumbling, and the children scatter. End of incident. Tomorrow Madame Margel is coming to get me. First we'll go to a tea room for creamy pastries. Then we'll spend a moment in the furniture store, and we'll finish the day with a delicious hot chocolate. There's no use rushing to believe bad news that probably isn't even true. What does the director know, anyway? I'm going to keep waiting.

—⁓—

I've been going to Madame Margel's house once a week for more than three months now. We have a great relationship. She's the first grown-up—except for my parents, of course—with whom I can laugh openly. We converse as equals. She never makes me feel how young I am. She asks me about my tastes, my ideas—in short, she respects me. We speak informally, and I even call her by her first name. I have an idea: since she seems to want a son so much, since we get along so well together, maybe she could get me out of the castle.

I take a deep breath and broach the matter: "Odette, I've been thinking about something. . . . Maybe I could come live with you. I've had enough of the orphanage."

"My dear Joseph, it's impossible. I can't adopt you."

"I don't want you to adopt me! If you do that, I'll lose my name, and my parents won't be able to find me. Instead, come for me every day, not just Sundays. . . ."

"Let me think about it. . . ."

The following week, the director of Méhoncourt is overjoyed when Madame Margel asks to take custody of me, which he obviously agrees to. Because he knows what I refuse to believe: my parents are never coming back from the camps.

—∼∼∼—

I like living at the Margels'. Convinced that I could have brilliant results in my studies—I can't imagine why!—Odette enrolls me in enrichment classes. I'm back in school, and for the first time in my life I can actually say I'm enjoying it. Maurice is fairly reserved at home. He doesn't talk much, probably because he doesn't speak French all that well. He doesn't realize how much I enjoy hearing him say a few words in Yiddish to me when he gets home from the store at night. It's my mother's language, and even if his voice is different from hers, his intonation and the tenderness he puts into each sentence take me back to the Rue des Abbesses.

The happiness doesn't last for long. After a few months, I come down with a high fever that I can't shake. The family doctor, finding no explanation for the state I'm in, sends me to the hospital in Le Mans, where they decide I have a raging infection: pleurisy, a disease of the membrane that protects the lungs. It's the last stage before full-blown tuberculosis. Too many privations over too many years have taken their toll on my health. No more family meals in the evening, no more daytime classes, no more Sunday afternoon walks. I'm trapped in bed and stuffed with vitamins while waiting for a bed to become free in a sanitarium.

It will be le Christomet, in Megève, high in the French Alps. Fortunately, the fever and my weak constitution leave me in a state of torpor. Up there in the mountains, every day is the same: a big breakfast, a walk in the fresh air, a meal rich in proteins and vitamins, then a four-hour nap in the solarium, two hours playing bridge or chess, dinner, and off to bed! Only my letters from Odette and Maurice break the monotony. On the other hand, I still have no news of my parents. I feel as though my life has been put on hold again by some kind of all-powerful force, unless it's simply a matter of chance.

I've been mothballed. My head and heart are numb. I don't hunger for anything, I have no desires, I don't even think about tomorrow or about my life as a man, which would be starting now if I were in better health. I just turned fifteen. In theory, I'm at an age when I could be starting in on a trade, old enough to be earning a living and seeing to my own needs. Other boys, in the city, flirt with girls, go to the movies, meet up to play cards or go dancing. As for me, I sleep all day. In any case, I'm not even sure that I would act like the others if I were back in Le Mans, at the Margels' or somewhere else. I didn't have enough of a childhood, and I doubt that I'll be able to make a big leap forward when I get out of the sanitarium. I'll always regret the happy memories that I've been unable to store up since the summer of 1942, and I'm afraid that I'll never be able to make up for lost time. And now I'm losing even more. . . . Here everything seems endless. . . .

My ordeal at Le Christomet lasts a year, the time they need
to decide not to keep a Jew there anymore. I have to say that
there are more and more signs of anti-Semitism inside the sanitarium. One day, while I'm looking at a painting a boy is working on—a real snob from the sixteenth arrondissement in Paris,
also recuperating—he sneers, "Get away from me, Jew! You're
soiling my work of art. . . . "

His "work of art"! What a jerk!

I have a very generous young priest who protects me, a child-
like guy who has only nice things to say. He's sick, too, and he
comes from the Sarthe, so we have things in common. Every
Saturday evening, I'm the one he entrusts with the task of pre-
paring the holy chapel for mass. I have to transform the game
room into a church for the next day—an opportunity to drink a
little glass of the wine reserved for the service. . . . One day, we're
receiving the archbishop of Paris. My priest puts on his most
beautiful cassock and explains to each patient how to behave
with our important visitor.

"You need to present yourselves to him, one after the other,
bend on one knee, and kiss his ring."

I take my place in line and take small steps toward Monsignor
Suhard, the very man who blessed the departure of the German
troops when they left Paris. As I begin to kneel, I feel a hand
grab me by the collar and eject me forcibly, with the comment,
"Not this one. He's a Jew!"

So they send me back to Le Mans—too bad if I'm not completely cured. Robert Jarry, future mayor of my city who was
also ill, suffered the same fate, but for different reasons: they
expelled him from the sanitarium because he belonged to the
communist party.

I learn about the gassings in the camps. But I also know that
some of the deportees have managed to return. I hear that they

weren't as well treated in Auschwitz and the other camps as I was in Beaune-la-Rolande. If they survived, I can surely get over this illness. . . . I still hope to see my parents and my sisters once again. I'm not as sure as I was right after the Liberation—doubt has set in, but I can push it out of my mind. I can't grasp for more than a few seconds that good, honest people like my parents were killed or that two innocent little girls were struck down only because they were Jewish. I'd feel a terrible sense of injustice if I could never hold them in my arms again, after all I've lived through since they were taken away. . . . No, I'm not going to think about the worst. In fact, I choose to believe the best, no matter what. And so I return to the Margels', happy to be able to live out my never-ending convalescence in the warmth of their home.

I want to state right now that ordinary anti-Semitism has continued here in Le Mans as well and shows its ugly face as freely as during the war. The Margels offer me the possibility of taking a Pigier course to learn accounting. When I arrive, the class has already been in session for several weeks, and I have to join a group that's been together for a while. The director doesn't introduce me to the other students, but I recognize one of them, the son of an important grocer in Le Mans, a big shot. Madame Margel and I ran into them one Sunday while they were taking a family stroll. She spoke to me about them, discreetly, from a distance. Only one seat is free in the classroom, next to this pedantic, proud, petty-bourgeois kid. The director apologizes. "Michel, I'm very sorry. I have to put this boy next to you. But I can promise you that it won't be for long."

He said "this boy," not "this Jew." Maybe I'm making progress. . . . A few months later, we take the final exam. I fail by a quarter of a point, while all the others pass. I must have made one error too many. . . . It doesn't matter. I'm sixteen, at the age when I can go to work. My path is laid before me: there's an office job waiting for me at the Margels'.

—~~~—

Maurice and Odette give me self-confidence, just as my parents would have if they had been with me over the last few years. They encourage me not to let any opportunity pass me by and not to be embarrassed to demand what I consider my due. I read in the newspaper that the FNDIRP, the Fédération Nationale des Déportés et Internés, Résistants et Patriotes, has decided to offer fur-lined jackets to former prisoners. Even if it's not that cold in the Sarthe, I dream of a soft, warm winter coat. . . . I report to the office of this generous organization.

I'm the youngest one there. When it's my turn, I hand them my identity card, the very one that the Fédération gave me a few months earlier. A man grabs it, looks at it attentively, and hands it right back to me. "Young man, you don't have a right to a coat. You weren't in a camp long enough."

I look at him in astonishment, and I can feel a violent anger boiling inside me.

"What do you mean, not long enough?"

"You have to have spent at least six months in a camp."

"Six months? I need to have been there six months? And I have to have taken the train with my parents, no doubt!"

"Precisely."

This man's calm attitude sends me over the edge. I don't even want to know if he understands how outrageous his remark is. I'm wild with rage.

"My parents and my two sisters were arrested on July 16, 1942. Maybe that date means something to you. You can probably figure out that I was with them. We spent five days in the Vélodrome d'Hiver. Then we were taken to the camp at Beaune-la-Rolande, in the Loiret—perhaps you've heard of that, too. We had nothing to eat and were treated like shit. Almost five years ago, I was able to escape from there, but my entire family was 'deported,' as they say. Today I have no idea what's become of them. I don't know if I'll ever see them again!"

While I'm shouting, several employees of the Fédération join us in the office, and the people waiting in line behind me approach us. The man I'm addressing doesn't even try to silence me. As I'm speaking, he suddenly seems to understand what I've been through, but most of all he's stunned by the force of my anger. It's true that I'm only sixteen, but I look fourteen, and someone my age isn't supposed to speak this way to an adult. In theory. But what do logic and good manners have to do with this situation? In itself, a fur-lined coat is nothing. In the end, I don't give a damn about this coat or about any other that I might even buy myself. No, in refusing me this coat on the absurd pretext that my ordeal wasn't long enough, this employee of the Fédération is denying purely and simply that the suffering I endured ever happened. He's drawing an X on this part of my life that I'm dragging around like a millstone. He's affirming that what I went through didn't exist or that it doesn't count, that I have no right to complain or to demand any sort of reparation. In short, that I'm not a victim. But what am I then? I leave with a coat a little too big for me. I can still grow a couple of inches, so it will always fit me.

——————

I have a very convenient character flaw: when I don't like the truth, I hide it from myself. It doesn't exist. In 1947, when I'm over my infection and almost serene and happy at the Margels', welcomed like a son, I learn what really happened once the trains arrived at their destination. The names have a less poetic ring than *Pitchi Poï*. Auschwitz, Sobibor, Treblinka, Chelmno, Majdanek. . . . All of these camps were in Poland. So, in the end, it's true that my parents went back to their native land. I listen to the radio and read the papers. Voices of sympathetic people around me tell me that they'll probably never return. They break the news to me gently, and I can see in their eyes the noble and generous intent to make me believe the truth while causing me the least possible pain. I hear them, but I don't listen to them. I turn my head and look away. What they tell me doesn't really affect me: I don't believe it. Horrors may have been committed, but they don't concern me.

Madame Margel could sit herself down in front of me, grab me by the shoulders and force me to listen to her without interrupting or looking away. She could say to me, "Joseph, I'm truly sorry. I've consulted the lists of prisoners drawn up by the Germans at Auschwitz. I know what day your parents arrived there, and I also know that they're not going to return." She could tell me, "I know how much this news must make you suffer, I know that I'm dashing all your hopes, but you have to admit the truth to yourself now. You have to give up your illusions and move forward." Only she doesn't say any of this, out of kindness to be sure. She probably thinks that, with time, each day that passes will help me get used to the idea that I'm an orphan, and that it's irreversible.

Mind-boggling numbers are put forth. People speak of millions. That seems simply impossible to me. And if I choose to believe it, to admit it, even for a tenth of a second, I fall into an abyss of despair. So I continue to doubt: it helps me to survive. It's an unconscious choice, but, for a time, I grant myself the benefit of the doubt. I don't contact any of the organizations that deal with survivors to find out what happened to the Weismanns. I've heard about the Hotel Lutétia, in Paris, where all the information about the victims of the camps was gathered after the war. I know that thousands of photos of persecuted Jews have been put up on the walls there. Maybe if I look at these pictures, one by one, I'll end up finding a photo of Papa, Mama, Charlotte, or Rachel. But what will the caption underneath tell me? The number of their train? What difference does the number make? Something else? I don't know what there is to know, but I prefer not to find out. It's still completely out of the question for me to give up the thought of my mother's tenderness.

Poor Odette must suffer terribly from my attitude. Without really pushing her away, I keep her at a respectable distance. I call her my aunt. That works for me. You love an uncle or an aunt. They're family. They have certain responsibilities toward their nieces and nephews. They can make decisions for them and even have the duty to help them if their parents can't. That's what Odette and Maurice represent for me: they're more than strangers, but in no way can I consider them my parents. Aunt and uncle will do just fine.

—⁂—

I have a fight with Odette and Maurice. Furious with them because they don't allow me the freedom I want, I wrap my belongings in a bundle and take the train to the capital, shouting a thunderous good-bye. I go to stay with Momo, an old friend from Le Mans, who counsels moderation without much success.

"Listen, Joseph. The Margels consider themselves your parents, but it's to protect you. It's because they love you."

"I don't care. They have no right to try to control me. I'm going to find some kind of job around here somewhere, and I'll be perfectly fine."

There's no way I can move in with my uncles, but I go to visit them anyway. Emile isn't really surprised to see me outside his door: Odette, convinced that I sought refuge with him, wrote him a letter. He shows it to me in the hopes of taking part in a reconciliation. She's sent him a true declaration of love, writing about how attached she is to me, the son she never had. She reminds me of how she gave me everything after she took me—still a child—out of the Castle of Méhoncourt. And she promises to give me whatever I could possibly hope for if only I'll come back. This outburst of love is terribly moving, and reading it is probably what leads me to make up my mind then and there: I'll stay with the Margels.

A similar letter is waiting for me at my Uncle Albert's. My mother's brother receives me as well, but he seems very embarrassed. In any case, I don't expect anything from him. When it's time for me to leave, he says, "I'm your uncle. I should take care of you." I also hear what he doesn't say—that he's not going to, never intended to, but that he's apologizing in a way. I quickly reassure him: "Don't worry. I'm OK where I am."

In the office of the furniture store, among the papers, I'm bored, but in the showroom itself, I work wonders. I know everything about how they make headboards, sofa beds, and three-door armoires with a mirror in the center. I talk up the merchandise with the customers with unbelievable self-assurance. I see Joe and me again after our escape, imitating bombardiers flying over Paris for the other kids who had bad intentions toward the two of us. In the Margels' store, I play the furniture expert with just as much conviction, as if my life depended on it. I understand that selling is like music: either you have a gift for it or you don't. I'm the Mozart of the kitchen hutch!

Too bad there's no Mozart for accounting in the office. . . . Maurice, convinced that every penny that comes in is profit, gives ridiculous contributions to charitable institutions. His generosity soon leads the store into receivership. Every week from now on, we have to bring the money we've earned to a financial organization that manages our business. The court has given us five years to become solvent. We all work like maniacs to meet this goal. Maurice has had tuberculosis for years, and unfortunately his health is deteriorating. He's suffered from a collapsed lung several times, and he's had just as many lung operations. He never complains about the physical suffering he must certainly be enduring and dies in his own bed on May 17, 1951, leaving Odette, his daughter, and me on our own. We bury him in the Jewish section of the cemetery in the presence of several members of the community. We're obviously grieving, but I don't shed a tear. What's happening here now pales in comparison to the tragic events at Beaune-la-Rolande. There's nothing I can do about it: everything brings me back to my past. Losing Maurice is certainly a difficult ordeal, and I'm sad that I'll never see him again, but as far as I'm concerned, I'm not losing a father.

During its convalescence, the business hasn't lost its owner, either. There's no question that Odette is in charge. I offer my aid out of love for this woman, whom I'm not going to be able to help for a year and a half: I have to leave in September for my military service. We keep only one member of the armada of salesmen she's hired, plus a secretary in the office and a deliveryman. In October, we'll have to pay the money we owe for the first due date established by the court. I've received a small sum of money from the state as compensation for what I've been through the past few years. . . . It will help me to pay off the debt when the time comes. Yes, I'm acting a little like the director of operations. But it's necessary, and Odette encourages me, just as she would a real son.

10 · Becoming French

The worst part is that I have to fight to be able to serve in the military. . . . I see my friends go off one after the other. First they're summoned by city hall. Then they undress at the *préfecture*, where the review committee decides if they're fit or not. The guys I met at the Pigier course are all found to be OK. Jacques is sent to Tunisia, and Michel goes to Morocco. Since no order comes for me, I decide to go to city hall to see why I've been left out.

I find myself face to face with a cheerless employee who obviously doesn't like to have to explain herself.

"Bonjour, Madame. My name is Joseph Weismann. I was born June 19, 1931, in Paris. I'm here to see you because I'm surprised that I wasn't called up for military service."

"Are you insinuating that I haven't done my job properly?"

"Madame, I'm not insinuating anything of the kind. I think I should do my military service like all the other boys my age, that's all."

"If you weren't called, there must be a reason."

I can guess what it is, but I prefer not to say anything. . . . I insist that I have to do my duty, and the employee gives in.

"Give me your address. You'll get a letter in the mail."

It doesn't take long for the letter to arrive: a week later I'm off to the base at Auvours, six or seven miles from Le Mans. During the three weeks I'm there for what they call "classes," I make friends with Guy, a young notary who could do without an adventure in the armed forces. I tell him that I went out of my way to sign up. He can't believe it. "What a crazy idea! If they forgot about you, you could have taken advantage of the situation and avoided all this."

I don't tell him about the Jewish boys—I know several—who tried to get themselves rated unfit for service because they were afraid the other guys in their barracks would be anti-Semitic. They knew that as soon as they took their first shower, they'd be identified as Jews and ostracized or even mistreated. Everything we went through in the war has left indelible marks on us, and for good reason. But I enlist in a different spirit. I don't want to hide anymore. On the other hand, I'm not looking for any special consideration, any favor—just to be treated like everyone else.

"Guy, I don't want them to say one day: *Those Jews. They want the same rights as the French, and they don't even do their military service.*"

"No one would say that! Not after what happened during the war."

"Don't be so sure. People's way of thinking hasn't changed. They'd bring it up whenever they could."

When classes are over, having learned how to march in formation, rifle over your shoulder, left, right, be on the lookout— the whole deal—Guy and I find ourselves in a train on the way to Cherbourg. The other guys, mostly from Normandy and Brittany, are leaving their villages for the first time. They're enjoying a new experience, freedom, and amuse themselves like kids at a carnival. The level of the conversation is pretty low. . . . I'm only a little furniture salesman and no intellectual, but really. . . .

One evening after our drill, a boy from Brittany, twice as tall as I and maybe twice as wide, orders me to tell all about myself. "You, Joseph . . . you're a Jew! You're gonna pay for a liter and tell us your story!"

"OK, bring on the glasses. But tell me first, what do you think a Jew is?" He's embarrassed by my question, but I don't let up. "You listened to the wireless during the war, right?"

He agrees reluctantly, almost with shame.

"So? You've seen me without my clothes on in the barracks. Am I a hunchback?"

"Uh . . . no."

"What about my nose? Do I have a hooked nose?"

"Of course not!"

"Do you want me to take off my beret so you can see my horns?"

"Hey, quit fooling around. . . . So, uh, you're just like the rest of us?"

"Of course."

When the Americans arrived in the Sarthe and I was with them every day, acting as guide or interpreter on the nearby farms, I never told them I was Jewish. I was still too ashamed. But things change over time. Now it's 1951, and I'm twenty. I've grown up and learned a lot. Historians have added up the numbers. They talk about millions of my people murdered for only one reason: they were Jewish. I've finally admitted that among these millions of human beings were a man named Schmoul Weismann, his wife, Sara, and their two daughters, Charlotte and Rachel. I waited for their return for nine years before I could accept the idea that it was never going to happen. It took a long time, but I made it. I cried many tears in secret in my bedroom at the Margels'. I reproached myself for having kept up my hopes for so long, but I congratulated myself just as much. If I had hoped so strongly for the return of my parents and my sisters, it's because I loved them and was loyal to them. Maybe I also felt guilty to be alive when they had all died. . . .

Whatever the case, when I felt ready to stand up to my army buddies about my origins, at age twenty, I was no longer ashamed to be Jewish. Now I feel an aggressiveness brewing inside me that I'm sure will never leave me. If the French hadn't swallowed all that propaganda so stupidly, if they had had a spark of curiosity sooner, if they had tried to find out for themselves, like my barracks mates today, whether the Devil was really incarnated in every Jew, the horrors in the camps would never have been committed.

———

As soon as they took me in, in 1946, Odette and Maurice tried to get me a French identity card. First they wrote to the town hall of the eighteenth arrondissement, in Paris, to get a birth certificate. Instead, what they found in their mailbox a few days later was a death certificate. Officially, I had been sent to Auschwitz with my parents and sisters, and my existence ended there. . . . When I came out of the sanitarium, I tried a different approach. Since no one in either the *préfecture* or the city hall of Le Mans seemed to have the wherewithal—or the desire—to sort out my situation, I decided to sue the French government. This caused me to come face to face with a judge who made this scathing remark: "Monsieur, not everyone who wants to be French can be."

Since my parents weren't born in France, I had to furnish proof that they had lived in Poland. Mission impossible: all the archives were destroyed during the war. The law states that you're born with your father's nationality, unless he requested to be naturalized French. That's my case: Papa applied in 1936 and was successful. However, Marshal Pétain revoked all naturalizations granted to Jews between 1920 and 1940.

Time passes, and one day I'm summoned to the *préfecture:* "Mr. Weismann, after examining your file we have decided to offer you a passport as a stateless person."

I return sheepishly to the Margels' and tell them the news. Maurice boils over in anger: "How dare they! After what they did to you! Don't accept it! You absolutely must continue to demand your French identity card. Don't stop bothering them until you get it. It's your right!"

So the file of Joseph Weismann, born June 19, 1931, in Paris, of Polish parents, continues to undergo examination for more than a year. It follows me to Cherbourg during my military service. Are they trying to put pressure on me to make me give up? In any case, every week I'm summoned to the police precinct, like a delinquent on probation, until finally, a few weeks before the end of my service, the police officer who receives me informs me of the public prosecutor's decision: "Mr. Weismann, your file is closed. You're not French."

With great pleasure, I play the fool: "Really? But . . . well, you see, there's a slight problem: I'm in the French army. For almost 18 months now. My service ends in two weeks. I didn't ask to be in the army, you understand. I was registered and declared fit. I took my courses, my service is almost completed, and I'm even being discharged as private first class."

"I see. . . . In that case, I'll transmit this information. . . ."

My eighteen months of service are over, and I leave with a good conduct certificate and the decoration preceding my promotion. It's just a wool stripe on my uniform that gives me no particular advantage or any authority over the other soldiers. I haven't spoken about my story to anyone. If I have to lighten my burden, it won't be to these people. I keep my deepest feelings to myself: my lost parents, my loneliness, even the fact that France, where I was born—France, which caused all my suffering—doesn't want me.

It's 1953, and I'm twenty-two. I have a new family, which now consists only of Odette, and an uncertain future in a shaky business. But still no papers. It's an unequal battle. Who's going to win, me or the government? I hire a lawyer to defend my rights. My military record works in my favor: in case of conflict, I can be mobilized. How could a judge deny that I'm French? The Ministère des Anciens Combattants acquired a certificate stating that "Monsieur Schmoul Weismann received his French citizenship in 1936 and never lost it." However, the original document has disappeared.

If I changed my name, if I suddenly were called Marcel Dupont, I certainly wouldn't have any problem obtaining my papers. So far, being Jewish has brought me nothing but unhappiness. If only I believed in my religion! If, like my mother, I at least placed all my hope in God, maybe I'd find some kind of consolation. . . . At the Castle of Méhoncourt, Jewish-American soldiers came to celebrate the major holidays with us. We sang the Hebrew national anthem in the evening. We could also attend religion classes, but I didn't go. The only thing Jewish about me is my name. I have the impression I'm paying for all the generations of Jews since Jesus Christ. At my birth, I received a fabulous inheritance: Judaism plus the right to be persecuted. But in the name of what? What does the settling of scores in the year 33 in Jerusalem have to do with a kid born in 1931?

I can still see the table in our apartment beautifully set for Passover. I didn't realize it at the time, but my mother must have deprived herself all year long to organize such a wonderful feast. She must have put aside penny after penny to thank God that day with such beautifully prepared food. Mama was overly observant. She believed too fervently. If God exists, if there was some meaning to being Jewish, He wouldn't have allowed her to be crushed like an insect. My mother laughed often. She laughed at my father's jokes and at Charlie Chaplin's comical behavior. She was a simple woman, sweet and kind, uneducated because she didn't go to school, but endowed with a lively, practical intelligence. She deserved her place on this planet. If she were here, at my side, to see me begin my adult life, I wouldn't deny the existence of God and I wouldn't see being born Jewish as a curse. I wouldn't be plagued with doubts. Everything I believed in disappeared with her, everything that I was due—her love, the love that every mother feels for her children. There are no words that can describe how I long for that love. Even if I love someone again, even if one day I am loved in return, it will be different. It will be important to me, but it will be nothing compared to Mama's love.

In Auschwitz, the girls and women's hair was carefully combed, then cut and wound into thread. It was made into slippers for submarine crews and felt socks for officers of the Reich. Could Mama's God have allowed that?

Now that my military service is over, I decide that it's time for me to take control of the business. "Odette, you and your husband have been poor managers, and you know very well that there can't be two bosses. So either I run things now or we sell the store and close down."

Odette immediately goes along with my plan. She's not a submissive woman who can be ordered around—on the contrary. But she is smart enough to recognize her limitations. Hand in hand, each as happy as the other at our new arrangement, we throw ourselves into three years of intense work. She trusts me to get the Meuble Parfait, a viable business, back on its feet. From now on, work is my whole life.

—✦—

I decide to leave for Israel, but not to go live there. And not to work the land that my mother dreamed of so much. I'm going to see Kaïla, Mama's sister. She's been doing research since the end of the war, found out that I survived, and wrote to me. I've seen this aunt—this real blood relative—only once. I was three years old, and Mama went to Poland to visit her. Apparently, during our entire stay, I didn't leave her side for a moment, taking her for a second mother because she looked so much like mine. She said in a letter that I even slept in the same bed with her.

Before boarding the boat for Israel, Kaïla wrote to me to join her in Marseilles. The letter arrived too late. In any case, I wouldn't have embarked with her: in 1948 I was still hoping to be reunited with my parents, and I couldn't have left France. Now that all is lost—and since my uncles Émile and Albert don't act like family toward me—I decide that I should at least go see Kaïla and hold her in my arms, in memory of Mama.

I'm totally shocked when I see her. I don't know what I was expecting. Kaïla looks exactly like my mother twelve years earlier, when we still lived in our apartment in Montmartre. She has the same laughing eyes, the same delicate mouth, and the same straight, little teeth. Her skin is just as dark and soft, and she also wears her hair in a bun, just above her neck. She has the same tender expression when she looks at me.

After the initial emotion has passed, we should be able to use words to communicate, but we can't. Kaïla speaks only Yiddish, and even though I can understand it pretty well, I have a hard time speaking it. During the ten or so days I spend with her, she's still able to transmit a few messages to me: my place is at her side from now on. The Germans took away my mother and left me my aunt as my only remaining relative. She'll love me like a mother. She tells me how proud she was the day her son was born: she remembered me, the son of her beloved sister, and now she had her own Joseph. The fact that I made it through the war alive when no one else did, either on her side or mine, seems to her to be a message from God: He's giving her back her son!

I have a certain amount of affection for this woman, but I'm afraid of disappointing her with the limited emotion I feel toward her. I ask her for a few days to think it over, while I travel around this new country to see if I can actually consider living here.

I'm given the address of a French kibbutz near Jerusalem named Neve Ilan. As soon as I take one look at it, it seems the most miserable place on earth. The young people who live there seem to have no idea why they're there and what they're supposed to accomplish. Everything is dirty and decrepit, and no one seems to have the will to improve the situation. So, no, I can't imagine living my life there.

Kaïla finds me another kibbutz, Kineret, right near the Sea of Galilee. She worked there for a few months when she arrived in Israel and thinks I could be happier there, although there aren't any French people. However, I do find one: another orphan from the Castle of Méhoncourt. He raises peanuts and enjoys his life in this paradise. Here everyone works, and the little village is prospering. The environment is very pleasant, with its groves of date palms, mango trees, and olive trees. The little gardens are beautifully cared for, and the few hundred families have dinner together serenely at the huge common table. The kibbutzniks, who all have fond memories of Kaïla, make me their guest of honor. Their kindness and the warmth of their greeting show me that I could find a place among them. But I really don't see myself there. Or not yet, anyway.

When I return to Kaïla's, I know that I'm going to break the last intact piece of her heart, but there's nothing else I can do. I have to explain to her why I can't live my life by her side in this land that Mama spoke of in all her prayers. First of all, in spite of what Kaïla says, I have another aunt waiting for me in France who needs me: Odette. She took me out of the Castle of Méhoncourt and offered me both a home and her love as soon as she could. I don't doubt that she would have done so right after I escaped in August 1942 if our paths had crossed then. I promised to help her save her store from bankruptcy. After all she's given me—most of all, her trust in allowing me to take over the business—the least I can do is see things through to the end.

Then I explain to Kaïla that I'm an adult now and no longer need the love of a mother. It's too late now, anyway—only my real mother could make up for lost time. And finally, my country is calling to me. I like Israel's golden hues, the smell of the orange trees and of the sea, but I already miss the green grass of France. I can't wait to experience another autumn, to see the leaves turn red, then yellow, and then to watch the wind blow them in every direction. I miss the *paupiettes de veau* and the wines of the Loire Valley.

My aunt asks me, "You don't feel as Jewish as I do?"

I tell her that I'm Jewish only by birth. I understand and respect the decisions of those who only want to live in Israel from now on. But I'm French, French first and foremost. I'm not afraid of my country or its inhabitants. I can stand on my own two feet and build my life. It's in France, and nowhere else, that I can imagine my future.

I return to Le Mans.

11 · Return to the Past

I can go for days and days without looking back. In the morning, I take my children by the hand and cover them with kisses before turning them over to their teachers. Then I walk joyfully to the store to join my colleagues. And the day goes by peacefully, its rhythm broken only by the sound of the bell when a customer walks through the door. . . . Happiness straight ahead, now and forever. Nevertheless, certain memories enter my mind without my calling them up. They appear out of the blue without announcing their arrival or taking into account the turmoil they can stir up and the damage they can do. I have a strategy for keeping them under control: I think about whatever slightly happy events occurred during the same time period, about the people who comforted me and helped me to keep my head high. I know, or rather I sense, that I need to find these people to reconcile myself with my past.

First of all, there were the two gendarmes who saved Joe and me by ordering that we be put in the bus for Montargis. The day before, they could have taken us back to the camp of Beaune-la-Rolande. Our clothing left no doubt that we were Jewish escapees. They knew to play innocent, to consider us as two harmless vagabonds. That way, in case we were recaptured by the Germans themselves, they could have at least saved their own skins and—who knows?—helped others like us afterward. The next day they gave further proof of their courage by coming to meet us at the bus stop and ensuring that our trip back to Paris continued with no problems.

Once again, that morning, they weren't very friendly: no one could have suspected them of helping Jews, which obviously was a risky business. But they did it, with dignity and without considering themselves heroes. They represent the France I love, whereas I feel an inextinguishable rage against that part of the population that, at best, showed indifference—and at worst, collaborated with the Germans by denouncing people. I'm going to find these two gendarmes and embrace them.

Unfortunately, when I try to locate them, I learn that they're dead.

Others helped me, especially in Paris. I've forgotten their names and addresses. They'll always remain kindhearted ghosts to me—I'll never get to hug them. There's one person, though, one person more than all the others that I'd like to see again: Joe Kogan. Without him, I wouldn't have dared to escape from Beaune-la-Rolande. In fact, I couldn't have done it with anyone else but him. Only Joe had enough out-of-the-box thinking, enthusiasm, and optimism to make this crazy attempt with me. We both lived through intense moments that determined our later lives—I wouldn't be here today if we hadn't succeeded together.

The day we went our separate ways at the Gare d'Austerlitz, I don't think we realized that we were linked together forever, even if we were never to see each other again. He went off to the twentieth arrondissement, and I rushed straight toward Montmartre. We barely even said goodbye, and if we exchanged addresses, it was basically for no reason at all: it was obvious that I wasn't returning to live my life peacefully at 54 Rue des Abbesses, going down every morning for my mail. Whatever happened to him? Was he recaptured or has he been as lucky as I have? Where is he living today—if he's still alive? Does he need help? Is he at least living a comfortable life with a roof over his head and enough to eat every day? If he's alone, I'd like to offer him support, shake his hand as I did in Beaune-la-Rolande to seal our pact, show him that I'm ready to help him out, as he did me.

Is it by chance that I find myself in Paris that day in 1965? Do I have to be in the city where I was born for the past to return? I've come there to make some purchases for the store. The furniture fair is on all week, a must for all dealers. I'm staying with my friend, Lucien. Every evening I return to his apartment, exhausted from the heat, the noise, and the incessant buzz of activity. I collapse in an armchair, we share an aperitif and a light supper, and I go to bed. But this night. . . .

The phone rings, and Lucien answers it. I see a quizzical look on his face. He turns to me to indicate that the conversation is about me.

"Yes, Joseph Weismann is here. I'll be glad to hand him the phone, of course, but please tell me who's calling."

Lucien is not an accommodating person. He can't put up with any lapse in good manners. "It's Mr. Weismann calling? Do you take me for a fool?"

Silence.

"All right, you can talk to him. But if this is some kind of joke, I can assure you that I don't find it at all amusing."

I take the receiver. My friend walks away, discreetly, shaking his head.

"Hello? This is Joseph Weismann!"

"Good evening, sir. Excuse me, I know it's a strange coincidence: My name is the same as yours—or almost. It's spelled with two *s*'s and only one *n* at the end."

"Yes? What do you want?"

"I'm calling on behalf of my cousin, Joe Kogan."

I signal to Lucien to pull over a chair. I think I'm going to faint.

"So . . . um . . . Joe is still alive?"

"He lives in America. He asked me to find you, and I'm happy I succeeded! He's spoken about you so often. . . . I'm in Belleville, in the twentieth arrondissement. Could we meet some time?"

"Don't move. I'm coming!"

As I mentioned, when I wrote to the town hall of the eighteenth arrondissement for my birth certificate, they sent me back a death certificate. Obviously, I immediately sent a letter explaining my situation, so that the information could be corrected and little Joseph brought back to life. It was in following the thread of this correspondence that Joe's cousin was able to find me. I had moved several times, of course, but my address and phone number were always in the telephone book. Weissman, with two *s*'s and one *n*, looked up my number—Le Mans 1698—and spoke to my wife. She gave him Lucien's number, and now here I am at a table, sitting face to face with a man who grew up with my fellow escapee!

He gives me a brief summary of Joe's life after our return to Paris. My friend went to his aunt's house. By sheer chance, she hadn't been arrested, and they remained in hiding together until the Liberation. Another aunt, in America, learned about Joe's story. She sent him a boat ticket so that he could join her and start a new life. Even better: she sent him two tickets. The second one was supposed to be for me. She felt that we were like brothers, and she wanted to welcome us both. But in 1945, I was still at the Castle of Méhoncourt, and the officials in Paris thought I was dead! When Joe Kogan's family tried to find me to propose that I emigrate to the U.S., their search was unsuccessful, and my friend crossed the Atlantic without me. He lives in Brooklyn, New York. At first he was a photographer. Now he works as an executive in a business that specializes in developing photographs.

I'm so happy that as an adult Joe wanted to know more about me. He could have been satisfied with what the town hall told him in 1945. After all, I could have been arrested again and sent to a camp later during the war. And what luck that his cousin has found me at this very moment. It just so happens that I have a plane ticket for Chicago via New York in my pocket. I'm going there in a month for a furniture convention.

When I finally call Joe two weeks before my trip to confirm my arrival, what a letdown! His wife tells me that he was just hospitalized for a fairly serious heart problem. I can't believe it: He's in danger of dying, twenty-three years after our crazy escapade, just when we're about to be reunited!

Fortunately, he recovers quickly.

Loneliness and absence have at least one advantage: They give a particular character to reunions. I was extremely moved when I met my aunt Kaïla in Israel, and I feel no less so in the hotel lobby in New York where Joe is waiting for me. His cousin showed me a photo of him, and I recognize him immediately. And he's able to recognize me from twenty yards away among all the people in the crowded hotel. We stare at each other for a few long seconds, and when we fall into each other's arms, it's as though we just escaped from Beaune-la-Rolande. What wonderful revenge to be reunited this way, two grown men, who'll always be orphans—two children who survived Nazi barbarity only because of their own courage!

We go to his apartment and spend the entire night telling each other the story of our lives. The next morning, I have to take the plane to Chicago for the convention, but the least I can do is take advantage of my stopover to learn about my friend's journey and tell him about mine. Joe obtained his American citizenship soon after his arrival and did his military service in his new country, in the photography division of the army.

"Imagine, I was sent to Germany!" he says. "It was the very beginning of the Cold War, and there were still a large number of American soldiers stationed in defeated Germany."

"Did you return to France on one of your leaves? Did you see any of your remaining family members in Paris?"

"Joseph, no one was left in Paris, and I didn't want to set foot there in any case. I was too young. I hadn't forgiven my country yet. . . . You know, I bear an intense grudge against the Germans, of course, but they lost the war and now they're paying the price. France, on the other hand. . . . When I was eighteen, I made up my mind never to return to the country that turned my parents and 75,000 other Jews over to the Nazis. All of these people had chosen to live in France. They had feared for their lives in their own countries, in Eastern Europe, but they thought that France would protect them. Not only didn't it, but it condemned us to death!"

Joe's father was Russian and worked in his country's merchant marine. When his ship stopped in Marseilles in the early 1930s, he decided not to get back on board. He went to Paris, where he already had relatives, got married, and had a son. . . . It's funny: When Joe speaks French, his mother tongue, he has an American accent now. His Paris street kid intonation has disappeared and has been replaced by a rubbery inflect⸱

He introduces me to his wife and daughter, Andy. He seems almost ready to come to terms with the country of his birth.

"Joseph, do you remember when you threw your beret outside the barbed wire in Beaune-la-Rolande? We weren't out of the woods yet! I was furious with you at that moment, but you really made me laugh, too. . . . I mean every time I've thought about it since then. . . . Listen, now that we've found each other, I'm going to go to France with my wife and daughter. You'll introduce me to your family, and we'll retrace our steps after August 1942, all of us together."

"Do you really think it's a good idea? It might stir up a lot of painful memories. . . . "

"We have to do it. And we'll be doing it together—that's the important part!"

———

There are pilgrimages that are no doubt unavoidable. . . . When I set out for the Loiret, with Joe, his family, and mine, I feel neither joy nor sorrow. Unlike all those years ago, when we were only kids with empty stomachs and broken hearts from being separated violently from our parents, Joe and I know this time how our journey will proceed. We leave without any worries and have a nice lunch in a restaurant. We'll stop in the places etched in our memories and then return home this evening.

I know that revisiting the villages that we passed through will bring me neither sadness nor satisfaction. But, to tell the truth, the trip will certainly be valuable—and not just for the two of us. My wife and children are often curious to know the details of what happened, and I've never told them the whole story. Every once in a while, at mealtime, I drop a few hints about my adventures. Francis, Nicole, and Isabelle, as young as they are, have a vague sense that the flames of some kind of powerful suffering are burning deep inside me. They have the instinctive delicacy not to press me when memories that rise to the surface bring tears to my eyes and reduce me to silence. They'll never know their grandparents, Schmoul and Sara, and they'll never have aunts or uncles, because my dear sisters are dead and Francine is an only child. We're their only relatives, and it's very important for them to know where they come from. I can at least show them the roads I traveled to become a man, then their father. The camp of Beaune-la-Rolande, like it or not, is also part of *their* story.

Nothing is left of it. They haven't left the slightest trace of the barracks, and certainly no hint of the barbed wire. It's a piece of public land, that's all. It's the mid-sixties, the war has been over for twenty years, but apparently it's not yet time to remember, not time for commemorations or tributes. Will that moment ever come? Will our elected officials understand, some day in the near future, the importance of marking an X on each place where a Jewish child was arrested, martyred, tortured? In France every trace is being erased instead.

The Vélodrome d'Hiver was torn down in 1959. When we were all jammed inside by the thousands, in July 1942, the people in the neighborhood saw us arrive. I found out later that they had to close their windows to prevent the foul odor emanating from the Vélodrome from entering their apartments. Our odor. . . . Of course, individually, these people couldn't have done anything. Alert the world? But whom, exactly, and how? All the means of communication were controlled by Vichy and the Germans. And what did the people of Paris know, anyway, about what we were suffering inside the Vél' d'Hiv? We ourselves didn't even revolt, out of fear and an excess of trust. Why would the residents of this fancy Paris neighborhood have taken the risk of simply asking a few questions? They closed their windows and waited for the wind and the rain to carry away the stench.

One thing astonishes me in Beaune-la-Rolande, when I think about it. To go from the station to the camp, we had to cross through the village. Those of us evacuated from the Vél' d'Hiv were certainly not the first people to walk down the main street, but we were definitely the largest number rounded up at one time to do so. I don't remember seeing any villagers as we were marched through. I was exhausted, of course, and my child's brain wasn't preoccupied by the thought of possible observers of our misfortune, but still: I don't remember seeing one face. Even if people were hiding behind their shutters—maybe they were afraid of Jews, since propaganda portrayed us as evil incarnate—they must have known how we were being treated. The fact that they weren't moved by the fate of the adults might be understandable, although. . . . But how could they have not batted an eyelash a few weeks later when it was children—and only children—disheveled, dirty, starving, obviously traumatized, who passed by their windows, returning to the station to be sent east?

I learned later on that the employees of the gingerbread factory had come to the gates of the camp to pass pieces of cake to the children. Apparently, the guards let them. Their action didn't save anyone, but at least it showed a bit of humanity.

Standing in the field that Joe and I had once walked across with the intense physical sensation that death was hot on our heels, I look at my two adorable daughters and my son. I imagine them in my place more than a quarter century ago and wonder. . . . They're neither more nor less beautiful than the 4,051 children confined in the Vél' d'Hiv and interned here afterward. They're children like so many others, like all others, Jewish or not. Of course, they're mine, and I love them more than anything else in the world, but even if I had no connection to them, I think, looking at them, that I'd still ask myself the same questions.

Without rancor, I turn to Joe, to share with him my endless inability to understand: "You know, Joe, we could repeat what happened a thousand times, tear up our scalps on the rolls of barbed wire, sleep in the woods, knock on doors that don't open—we'll still never be at peace. Because we'll never ever stop wondering why it all happened."

We continue our visit, each of us experiencing different emotions: Francis, Isabelle, and Nicole play with Andy, Joe's daughter, while our wives seem to understand for the first time what we lived through. We stop at the gendarmerie the woman took us to that night, and we cry in the tramps' hole, where the two kindly gendarmes sheltered us. We move on to the village of Lorris. It was there that Joe first thought we could find refuge; there that the family with whom he had spent his vacations a few years earlier offered us some soup before sending us back out into the night. We find the mother and the son. We didn't warn them we were coming, but they seem genuinely happy to see us. They even open a bottle of champagne! In 1942, I couldn't accept the fact that they had thrown us out. I found them cruel and cowardly and was furious at them. I don't harbor bad feelings toward them today. They live isolated in a little village house. They must have lacked everything during the war, bread but also information, and it's obvious that they didn't realize the danger we were in. You see, I keep coming back to the same point: either people had no way to know or they preferred to close their eyes.

Finding Joe again after all these years offers me more than just a return to the past, to the four days we spent together fleeing

Beaune-la-Rolande. All of a sudden, I have a better understanding of who I am. I feel as though I'm an outside observer, as if I'm someone else who's being introduced to Joseph Weismann, a man who doesn't talk much about painful things. . . . The moment Joe and I separated outside the Gare d'Austerlitz, part of me locked itself away behind the Joseph Weismann that people know. I never allowed myself to cry on anyone's shoulder, not Odette's or even my wife's. It's only now that I realize it, because this pilgrimage with Joe puts me face to face with another way of looking at life: my fellow escapee's.

In August 1942, seated side by side in the train taking us to Paris, we were in exactly the same situation: separated from those we loved, terrified at the idea of being recaptured, eager to find a place to survive, like two hunted animals searching for a hole where they can be forgotten. Was Joe luckier than I? Probably, because he didn't experience going from one orphanage to another, the roundups of children, foster families that weren't exactly welcoming. . . . But, all things considered, he was an orphan, too. In response to everything that happened to us, we've both followed the same course of action: happiness, happiness, happiness!

Nevertheless, we've developed different attitudes. I could see that when we entered the home of the woman who had thrown us out. He really didn't seem to be troubled. Joe doesn't burden himself with negative thoughts, sadness, or questions. Soon he's leaving New York for Las Vegas. The climate will be better for his heart. He's already delighted with the possibility of having a great time there, of welcoming us, of taking me to a casino. . . . Joe doesn't worry much about what's happening in the world. He chooses not to pay too much attention to things that don't touch him personally, and he says so loud and clear. I, too, thirst for happiness and try to cultivate positive thinking. But inside I'm suffering, and I remain silent.

I've done myself harm all on my own. I've alienated people who could have helped me to take a step back from my own story and that of the Jewish people. I've locked myself away in my childhood traumas. Since 1942, I've lived under a glass dome. A friend I've known for years was astonished recently when I told her what happened to me during the war. "Joseph, you never told us. You've always been friendly, smiling, cheerful; you joke a lot, but you've actually never spoken to us about yourself!"

She was right, and she made me realize it with great empathy. She would have liked to offer me the slight comfort that an attentive ear, a sincere and sympathetic friend, can provide. But why would I open myself up to her and not my other friends? Since I was eleven years old, I've kept my feelings to myself. At an age when I should have been coming out of myself, making my way in the world with confidence, I withdrew into myself the way a snail retreats into its shell. No one was there to explain life to me, and I had to find the answers myself to the questions everyone inevitably asks as he's entering adulthood. So what could I have told others, and how? "Hey, Claude, you want to go out for a drink Saturday night? I'll tell you about my short stay in the Vél' d'Hiv..." or "I just bought a silk camisole for my fiancée. Say, that reminds me of what the woman was wearing when the militiamen were kicking her in the ribs in Beaune-la-Rolande...."

Just as suddenly as Joe reappeared in my life, my first cousin found me. I don't remember ever having heard of his existence before the war.... Mikael is the son of one of Papa's brothers who didn't emigrate from Poland to France in the twenties. He chose to stay in Lublin before finally fleeing to Russia. Today Mikael lives in southern Poland and often travels, especially to France. Once, while visiting his aunt on his mother's side in Paris, he went to the Association of Children of Lublin to ask if anyone knew his uncle, Schmoul Weismann. As it turned out, Émile, Mama's brother, was the secretary of this organization.

"Do I know the Weismanns? Of course! Sara was my sister. Unfortunately, she was sent to the camps with Schmoul and their children. But one of them, Joseph, survived. He lives in Le Mans now, where he has a furniture store. Here's his telephone number."

When Mikael calls me, speaking in a mixture of Yiddish and German, I think I'm going to have a heart attack. A cousin . . . what a shock! Papa had spoken about his brother, never about his nephew. But what joy for me: even if this man lives in Poland, even if we might end up not really liking each other, he's part of my family, my blood. I don't hesitate for a moment. "I'm closing the store in an hour. Then I'm getting in the car and meeting you in Paris."

We spend the whole night talking in his aunt's apartment in Belleville. My cousin tells me his story, hardly any happier than mine. . . . He had to flee Lublin to escape the pogroms. In Russia, he was able to enroll in a middle school. He got his diploma and joined the army. As a Pole, and a Jew moreover, he had to fight to be able to enlist. . . . He received the Medal of the Order of Stalin for having participated in the liberation of Berlin. After the war he moved to East Germany, where he worked as a librarian, then to Denmark, where he became a citizen before returning to his native land. He speaks Yiddish, German, Russian, Danish, and, of course, Polish. The little bit of Yiddish I remember from my mother allows us to understand each other.

Mikael knew our common grandfather very well. When he speaks to me of him, I regret even more never having contacted him. "He was a very sweet man. Tall, more than six feet, and brave! Imagine, he joined the czar's imperial guard at age seventeen, even though the czar was a notorious anti-Semite. He was rewarded for his loyal service with a modest income that he put to good use: He got a hot sausage cart. Sometimes I joined him in his wanderings. He pushed his cart from village to village, and everywhere he went he told stories...."

When Poland was invaded in 1939, Mikael's father left for Russia all alone. He was a high-ranking member of the Bund (socialist party) and was advised to escape Poland before Germany invaded. In tears, my cousin tells me the terrible story of how he went to join him, when he was only fourteen years old.

"My parents had gotten divorced, and my father started a new life. I had a brother, Nathan, twelve years old, and a half-brother from my father's second marriage, Zev, age two. The persecution had grown much worse in Poland. They were killing Jews everywhere—in the street, all over the place. They forced them out of their homes, women, babies, old people, everyone. They stood them against a wall and *bang*—it was all over. One day, my father, in Kiev, decided we should leave. Little Zev, his mother, and I, set off for Russia, driven by a farmer in his small, wooden, horse-drawn cart. Nathan ran after us, begging us to take him with us, but his mother wanted him to stay with her in Poland.

"We drove to the River Bug and made a perilous crossing in the cart into Russia. Once we were on the other side, the farmer left us, and I carried baby Zev on my back through the dark night eleven miles to safety. Shortly afterward, Nathan, his mother, and the rest of their family who stayed in Poland were murdered by the Germans. My father eventually died in a Siberian gulag."

Imagine living with the knowledge that you could have saved your brother. Breathing, eating, drinking, singing, making love with this guilt forever in your heart. . . . How many Jews who returned from the camps committed suicide years after the war? Hundreds. It's ironic: all the Jews who survived the Holocaust feel guilty to be alive when they think of those who weren't so lucky. Mikael named his own son Nathan after the brother he couldn't save. He carries his terrible history with him, like so many others who day after day drag around the dark, heavy, dense burden of a tragedy both unique to them and universal. Nevertheless, we humans are marvelous beings: we can forgive—in any case, Mikael can. In spite of the anger and sadness stirring inside him, he has forgiven. Not me.

My cousin and I can spend two years without seeing each other, but we always stay in contact. We write each other and even call from time to time. Thanks to Mikael I feel much less alone, and for good reason: After the war, his father, my uncle, had another son and a daughter. Zev, the brother Mikael was able to save, moved to the U.S. and had three children. All these cousins consider me a member of their family. I'm once again part of a family tree, the Weismanns, and I'm not the only one producing new leaves. As the years go by, I'll be able to visit them in Spain, Florida, California, and Israel. I'll go to see them all and hug them. I'll keep up with their lives. There will be weddings, births, meals to share, fishing, sickness and many other problems as well, but we'll experience all these events, happy or sad, together. We're a family, and it's a wonderful feeling!

It's thanks to them, no doubt—because they exist and accept me as one of their own—that I'm able little by little to come out of my shell. I confide more often in my relatives. Nevertheless, I keep one secret: I don't tell anyone about an idea for a trip that's running through my mind.

A vague feeling has been growing inside me for years. It's not one that compels me to tell my loved ones the story of my childhood so I can relieve my pain; instead, it's calling me somewhere else: to Auschwitz, where my parents and sisters, like all the others rounded up in the Vél' d'Hiv, went to end their lives. I can't understand why, but it suddenly seems to me that I'll die of shame if another year passes without my going there. I owe it to my parents and my sisters. I have no choice.

My friends, including Joe, try to convince me not to make this macabre pilgrimage. They think that it will only reawaken my trauma, that I'll end up regretting it for the rest of my life. I don't listen to them, but it's true that I don't feel up to making the trip alone. Finally, I ask my cousin to go with me—I make it a condition of the journey. "Mikael, I feel the need to go to Auschwitz, but I'll only go if you come with me. Think about it. It'll be an opportunity for me to see where you live and to meet your wife and son. . . . "

He tells me to meet him in East Berlin. It takes a long time to get there in a Peugeot 404. . . . Francine and I don't stop to sightsee in France or Germany: we stop to rest and eat when we need to, but we're not in the mood to be tourists. The sixties are almost at an end, but not the Cold War. . . . Here we are in Berlin, at the mythical Checkpoint Charlie. I say mythical because beyond the wall, another world begins. Fear of the unknown produces all kinds of fantasies: Everything we've heard about East Germany has portrayed it as a country of misery, silence, and repression, infiltrated by the CIA under the guise of ordinary citizens, its secrets protected by the KGB. . . . Not everyone there is part of an intelligence network, of course, but we still have to provide proof that we're visiting a family member and indicate the date of our return. Our car is inspected with a fine-tooth comb, and our passports are examined for a long time by tense, distrustful, armed men. . . . Mikael is waiting for us on the other side. We've seen each other three times before this, always in France, proof that it's possible to cross the Iron Curtain—at least for him, a cultivated Pole and an elected official of his village.

When we cross the border, leaving opulent West Germany for East Berlin, we're immediately struck by the sinister atmosphere. While I'm physically retracing my parents' footsteps, my mind feels as though I'm going back in time.

Before taking us to Poland, my cousin wants to show us the city of Gera, in Thuringia. It's there that Hitler made his first show of force, in 1931. A few years earlier, he had already come to give a speech in this city bisected by a river. It took him hours to cross the bridge leading to the main square, because demonstrators blocked his way. After having convinced thousands of people to join his movement, Hitler returned to Gera, certain that this time he could easily crush any possible opponents. Not only did he attract crowds in the city to hear his new speech, but he organized a parade of 5,000 young Nazis in uniform, marching precisely in unison, as though they were part of a national army already set up and trained for many months, in spite of the fact that he wasn't even in power yet. How could the inhabitants of this region—how could the German people—doubt that this little, resolute man had been sent to them by Providence to save their country?

We take the car and head toward Auschwitz. We drive along the tracks used by the trains that systematically transported the victims here. The metal poles, all around the camp, are still standing perfectly straight. Their tops are slightly curved and each ends in a goose-neck lamp. On each pole there's a kind of socket with barbed wire wound around that is then stretched to the next pole.

We go in, and I see wooden barracks, bedsteads like rabbit cages, even narrower than those at Beaune-la-Rolande, mountains of suitcases, mountains of shoes, mountains of food cans—the internees' dishes—mountains of spoons, forks but no knives, mountains of blond, brown, and red braids, ponytails, buns still rolled up. A gas chamber with a tile floor and several holes drilled in the ceiling. Ovens. Several rooms have been made into a museum. The walls are covered with photos. I can see a woman, getting out of a cattle car, a child in her arms and another gripping her skirt. A man driving a backhoe, a cigarette between his lips, as if he were plowing his field at the end of the summer. He is in fact gathering the bodies, by the dozens. A child, emaciated and almost naked, is walking along an embankment where other children lie dead.

Next to us, tourists share a bottle of Coca Cola, as if they're on their way out of a movie theater.... It's good that Auschwitz-Birkenau has been preserved and transformed into a memorial. The Poles were right to do that. But for me, visiting this place is simply unbearable. We get back in the car, and I feel as though I've gone crazy. We drive without saying a word. I stop in a gas station to fill up, open the tank, and watch the employee start the pump. I'm shaking all over. I light a cigarette, and the employee begins to make wild gestures, shouting that smoking's forbidden, in Polish, which I understand so poorly. But of course, what an idiot I am.

"Mikael, where would you like me to drop you?"

"Listen, Joseph. You're overwhelmed. Please come rest at my house."

"Impossible. I can't stay in this country one more second."

We drive nonstop to Holland. We spend the night there and then go straight back to Le Mans.

I could never have looked at myself again in the mirror if I hadn't made this trip to Auschwitz. My decision was not based on logic: it was the result of an overpowering need. Just like when I escaped, I *had* to do it. Once again, I didn't shy away— I showed no cowardice. I look at my children and think about the ones I saw in photos there. So they weren't all exterminated the moment they arrived. It's horrible to say, but I hope with all my heart that my sisters were led directly from the train to the gas chamber. Why would I hope that they survived a week, a month, a year? What odor could the air they breathed have had? What could the bread they ate have tasted like? I sincerely hope that my parents were executed as soon as they got there. I could find out, perhaps, if I did some research. The Germans were very meticulous record-keepers. I don't want to know. I saw—that's enough.

Epilogue: Bearing Witness

For a long time I hid my feelings. Once my thunderous fit of anger was over—to get the fur-lined jacket being offered to French camp victims just after the war—I clammed up. If a friend suddenly asked me, "What about your parents?" my terse reply was "Auschwitz." I'd bend my head, and the person I was talking to would go on to another subject. It had to be a friend, of course. People who have no particular affection for you are rarely embarrassed by your distress. Their shameless questions are intended only to satisfy their curiosity, and they feel no compassion afterward. How many times have I controlled myself from sending them packing? And how many times didn't I control myself?

In the store, if I refused to give a big enough discount, for example, a customer would insult me. As stingy as a Jew, obviously. Or rather a kike, with two little kike daughters, as a parent said, according to what Francine and I were told too late after the incident for me to react. I would have gladly let loose my rage at the imbecile who uttered such an insult without thinking. Would anyone dare talk about "niggers" in the class? Fortunately not, but it took a long time for the words "nigger" and "Negro" to disappear from white people's uninhibited vocabulary. How much longer do we Jews have to wait?

The author Israel Shamir maintains that the Jew carries anti-Semitism inside him. That he creates it, in short, by his behavior and his beliefs. His words are so virulent that the Palestinians use them as part of their propaganda. I'm far from thinking, like Shamir, that we're responsible for causing the rejection that has brought us so much suffering. But I do wonder about a few things.

For a long time, Jews would invite only people from their own community to their homes. Their dishes became impure if they were soiled by mixing milk and meat. I remember that Mama herself broke a dish in a thousand pieces one day in the spring of 1942. We had nothing to eat, and the only product available with our rationing tickets was ham. . . . Mama didn't get flustered. She served us the meat and heaved a sigh of relief because that day her son and daughters at least had something to eat. But she gritted her teeth the whole time and then threw down the plate violently. Mama, so pious, didn't forsake her children that day. But she didn't renounce her faith, either, even though she didn't have two cents to buy another plate. I can't help thinking that maybe, in the twenties and thirties—even the forties—if the Jews had been more discreet in observing their customs . . . I don't know. Maybe the same horrors would have been committed anyway.

We were considered inferior beings, and we believed it—at least the children did. For a long time I remained silent because I was convinced I belonged to the Untouchable caste. Fortunately, I didn't adopt the opposite point of view, believing myself to be superior because I was Jewish. I became a "normal" person—that is to say, like other people—one who's pleased with his good choices and admits and regrets his bad ones. Today I have completely removed from my mind any idea of belief in God or of belonging to any religion. I base my decisions on logic, maybe not with great intelligence, but with common sense. I just turned eighty, yet I still have no certainties and no answers. But I've stopped remaining silent.

I spoke about my past for the first time in Orléans. It was there that I met Simone Veil, who joined the Resistance when she was only sixteen and was sent to Auschwitz with her mother and her sisters. She was arrested late in the war, in 1944, and owes her survival only to chance: she lied about her age so she could be selected to work. I felt admiration for this woman, of course, but not more than for any other member of the Resistance, Jewish or not. Being seated next to her didn't impress me. However, I quickly understood what made her an extraordinary woman.

First she asked me a question, discreetly, just before the conference began. "You often tell your story to others, don't you?"

I was truly taken aback. "Um . . . no, not really. Why?"

"Mr. Weismann, it's your duty to bear witness."

You have to have a lot of charisma to pull an old man like me out from the wall of silence he's lived behind for fifty years! Coming from anyone else, this statement would have provoked violent rejection on my part. But Simone Veil suffered the same things I did, since she lost her parents in the camps. In fact, she suffered even more because she was present at the death of her mother, exhausted and sick, and still had to summon all her strength every morning at dawn to go transport stones from one part of the camp to another. . . . Simone Veil's remark was warranted: I did need to talk about what I had suffered. Until then, I had preferred to remain silent—so as not to suffer from reliving difficult moments through words, no doubt, but not only for that reason. I was conscious, and I still am, that my story is no more or less important than that of the six million murdered Jews. It's different, that's all.

In the early nineties, a short time after meeting Madame Veil, I told my story to Blanche Finger and William Karel. They were doing research on the Vél' d'Hiv and looking for survivors who could describe the facts just as they experienced them, or as they remembered, in any case. They gathered their words verbatim in a book entitled *Operation Spring Wind*, the code name used by Vichy for the roundup. Joe Kogan and I told about crawling under the barbed wire, fleeing through the woods of the Loiret, the gendarmes. . . . I noticed a few differences in our accounts, inevitable so many years after the events. We should have written everything down right after our return to Paris, in August 1942. But we had other things to do. . . .

To publicize Finger and Karel's book launch, a half-century after the roundup, Jean-Marie Cavada produced a TV special. Léa, my little Léa, watched it. She jumped for her phone, was able to reach the producer's office, and was given my number. We reunited with enormous emotion. Physically, she was the woman one would have predicted during her childhood: little and slight. Her character, however, definitely had asserted itself! Léa is lively, chatty, and cheerful. She's lived an incredible life, a lot of it in the United States, where she worked as an acrobat for the Barnum and Bailey Circus. She's been married twice but has no children—by choice, she says. She didn't want to take the risk of having a Jewish child who could be afflicted with as much misery as she suffered. Judith, her sister, followed the same career path. They never left each other's side, and their family even grew: Their mother separated from their father shortly before the war and started a new life. . . . She gave birth to a third daughter whom she was able to hide, Annie. Completely by chance, both my adoptive sisters' parents were sent to the camps in the same train. They never returned.

Once again, thanks to the TV show, several children from the different orphanages I was in contacted me. In Lamarck, Rothschild, and the Castle of Méhoncourt, I wasn't really close to anyone, but I did have some friends. Of course, we didn't have many happy memories in common.

The teacher who worked in the old lady's village invited me to visit. It was fascinating to talk to someone I knew who was already an adult when I was as a child. Far from providing answers to the questions I asked myself, he raised others. He told me that he had no idea there was a Jewish boy in his class! When I arrived in 1943, without my parents, he didn't wonder what had become of them. According to what he said, no one, absolutely no one, in the countryside had any idea what was happening to the Jews.

It's true that in the 1930s, when the exodus of Jews began after Hitler's accession to power, few Poles or Russians, if any, moved to his village. Families settled in Paris and in the other big cities of France to be close to one another and help each other out. With no land, no trade sometimes, incapable of speaking French correctly, how could they have survived in a rural environment? I'd like to think that today, the Sarthe, where I live—the region I love so much—would know how to welcome foreigners. . . .

———

Now, as Simone Veil advised me, I bear witness, I fulfill my duty. I go regularly to convey my message to middle schools and high schools that invite me. Each time, it's hard for me to talk about our arrest, our confinement in the Vél' d'Hiv—and about the moment when I was torn away from my family. Standing in front of the children, I try as hard as possible not to cry, but I often see tears welling in my listeners' eyes. . . . Often, at the end of these events, they write to me, and I get the most satisfying reward. They tell me how touched they were but, most of all, they give voice to what they've understood—that this must never happen again. That's the main goal of what I'm doing. It does no good for me to tell my story just to make them cry. There's no benefit to humanity in that. I encourage them to reflect and, if necessary, to act.

When the children are listening to me, the look in their eyes makes me feel calmer. Certain other happy events have that effect as well. In the spring of 2010, three million people went to see *La Rafle* (*The Roundup*), Rose Bosch's film that relates what happened at the Vél' d'Hiv and at Beaune-la-Rolande. Ms. Bosch based much of the film on my story. She found an adorable, convincing boy, Hugo Leverdez, to play me. I also took part in the filming. When I entered the reconstituted Vélodrome, a putrid odor choked me. I walked out immediately and said to my daughter Isabelle, who had accompanied me, "What a horrible stench! How is it possible?"

She stared at me with her eyes wide open: "But Papa . . . there's no odor!"

Plunged into the sinister setting that I knew sixty-six years earlier, I somehow called up the memory of the unbearable smell that permeated the Vélodrome. . . .

When I attended the preview of the film, I didn't see anything. I relived the whole experience from inside and was completely incapable of telling Rose what she wanted to hear—that she had done a good job. Yes, she did. She showed the hate, the madness, and the stupidity in the eyes of the French civil servants who organized the roundup. Most of all, she showed the intolerable suffering of the 12,884 people arrested in Paris and in the surrounding area on the sixteenth and seventeenth of August, 1942. 12,844 is the official number—definitive, indisputable. There were 3,031 men, 5,802 women, and 4,051 children. Including my sisters. And me.

Me, lucky in the end because I survived. At the conclusion of the film, little Joseph escapes, a lot more easily than Joe Kogan and Joseph Weismann in real life, but what difference does it make? He escapes, and anything can happen to him after that.... After *La Rafle* came out, dozens and dozens of people, who recognized me from having seen me on TV or in the newspapers when the film was being publicized, asked me one question: "What happened afterward?"

Here's my answer. Afterward, I was loved or rejected. I often cried, but I looked for happiness in the most remote corner where it could be hiding, and I was able to find it. And I imposed a new trial upon myself, the duty to bear witness. I owed it to my parents, to my two sisters, to Joe, and to the 75,000 French and all 6,000,000 victims of Nazi barbarism.

There you have it: the story of a little boy growing up in Paris in a Polish family. He's poor but receives a lot of love, every day.... He goes to school, has friends, and doesn't ask himself many questions. In short, he's happy, until....

I realize that a book is something fairly inconsequential. But my grandchildren, whom I cherish, will read it. They'll talk about it with their friends, who, in turn, will perhaps speak of it to their families. Just as I have given up trying to understand how and why such horrors could have taken place, they'll eventually give up as well. But after having listened to my voice and to those of others who decided to speak out like me, they'll know. And all their lives they'll do their best to *make sure* that History doesn't repeat itself. At least that's my hope.

RICHARD KUTNER is an independent literary translator.

JOSEPH WEISMANN is a survivor of the Vél' d'Hiv Roundup (Paris, 1942). His story inspired the French film *La Rafle* (2010).

CPSIA information can be obtained
at www.ICGtesting.com
Printed in the USA
BVOW04s1340200417
481802BV00001B/2/P